# Inquiry-Based Psychotherapy:
# Applying The Work of Byron Katie in Clinical Settings

# Inquiry-Based Psychotherapy:

## Applying The Work of Byron Katie in Clinical Settings

Anil Coumar, MBBS, MA

Printed in the United States of America
First Printing, 2024

ISBN: 979-8-9901074-0-3

Anil Coumar, MBBS, MA
anil@coumar.net
www.coumar.org

# Inquiry-Based Psychotherapy:

## Applying The Work of Byron Katie in Clinical Settings

Anil Coumar, MBBS, MA

Printed in the United States of America
First Printing, 2024

ISBN: 979-8-9901074-0-3

Anil Coumar, MBBS, MA
anil@coumar.net
www.coumar.org

*To all my clients, past and present. Your courage, vulnerability, and resilience inspire me. Thank you for the lessons you've taught and continue to teach me.*

*Who would you be without your story?*

# FOREWORD BY DR. RAO

As the world emerges from the COVID-19 pandemic, many of us have realized that we have all been through a significant, psychological trauma. The consequences have been felt deeply, not only from loved ones lost to the illness, but also from the long-term impacts resulting from lockdowns and accompanying social unrest. The social isolation alone has had far-reaching impacts on the mental health of populations, often stemming from blockages in interpersonal communication and difficulties seeing people's body language. There is only so much that can be conveyed in a few words over social media, emails, etc., which have been our primary sources of communication since the pandemic. We've all noted instances of family members, friends, and colleagues jumping to extreme conclusions, judgments, and interpretations with little evidence for those jumps. We've all noted the accompanying uptick in anxiety, depression, suicidal ideation, and substance use, often resulting from misunderstandings and misinterpretations of social cues. These are the reasons why this book, Dr. Anil Coumar's practical advice on using Byron Katie's approach called, The Work, is so timely. We have a desperate need to re-introduce the psychological skills we had before COVID-19, before the isolation, before the social media onslaughts. This book, and The Work, will guide us towards how to find the evidence for drawing the conclusions that we do, how to question our assumptions and entrenched thoughts, and how to find a way to let go of these things that make us less able to experience joy in our lives.

Although many academic psychotherapists have a preferred technique they use, or have familiarity with one approach based upon training experiences, experienced psychotherapists know that we must keep an open mind to learning new techniques and tools. We know that one size does not fit all—some clients take to cognitive behavioral approaches, while others appreciate the social support strengthening provided by interpersonal therapies. Skilled psychotherapists know that we do not know our clients' experiences well enough to be too prescriptive with our approach to psychotherapy. We do know what works: when we start noting our clients reporting that their thoughts-behaviors-feelings—the cognitive triangle—have improved, then we know our approach is working well. The Work is cognitive-behavioral at its core, with its 4 questions (Is it true? Do you absolutely know that it is true? How do you react when you believe that thought? Who would you be without that thought?) that help our clients question their assumptions, and the turnaround, where clients develop the opposing thought. As Dr. Coumar tells us, The Work has the flexibility to stand alone or be paired with other approaches.

Then, of course, there is the matter of diverse clientele that we see outside of office settings, in schools, in primary care clinics, and beyond. I have worked in many non-psychiatric settings over the years, both domestically and internationally. My community and research partners have always asked for approaches that are brief, and often, familiar to the client. We often neglect to consider our social ties and cultural practices as therapeutic, but they are. Our social ties and cultural practices are often the first things to be dropped when we lack time and energy, balance multiple demands on us, in our increasingly capitalistic societies. My Indian colleagues often ask for deep breathing, yoga, and mindfulness to be re-integrated into our therapeutic approaches. The Work lends itself well to clients and therapists who cross cultural boundaries. In the Global North, our perspectives are influenced by Cartesian Dualisms—'I think therefore I am,' while in the Global South, we note the oneness of the mind and bodily sensations. Dr. Coumar links The Work reactions that are tied to our thoughts, feelings, behaviors—and our bodily sensations. I was struck by the similarity of The Work to South and East Asian philosophies, those rooted in Buddhism and Hinduism, particularly the teachings of Ramana Maharishi, where we question "who we are without our thoughts?"

Over the years, I have referred many of my students, friends, and colleagues to Dr. Coumar, particularly for his open mind, his kindness, and his humble approach to his clients. I have only heard positive things about their outcomes. Dr. Coumar's favored approach may not have the same 'evidence base' that other approaches do, but many of us who work in global mental health know very well about the biases inherent in the funding of behavioral interventions. All of these factors: our collective need to recover from COVID-19's isolating impacts, The Work's flexibility and applicability, my respect for Dr. Coumar, and its cross-cultural appeal, have guided me to keep an open mind in learning new techniques. I'm very happy to recommend this book, and the approach of The Work, to my friends and colleagues.

Deepa Rao, Ph.D., MA
Licensed Clinical Psychologist
Vice Dean for Faculty, School of Public Health, University of Washington
Professor, Department of Global Health

# FOREWORD BY DR. JACOBS

My personal connection to Anil Coumar goes back many years. When I met Anil in the late 1980s, he was at a professional turning point. Pivoting from the practice of general medicine to more direct provision of mental health services, he refocused his professional goals and sought training as a mental health counselor. Simultaneously, I completed training in psychology at the University of Washington and developed my practice to serve children, youth, and families. I recognized in Anil a shared commitment to alleviating the suffering brought on by mental health challenges. A friendship based on these shared interests began. Over the intervening years, I have been impressed by Anil's qualities which can be seen in this book: a keen intellectual curiosity, passion for learning, discernment, and intensive self-reflection. Anil's commitment to reducing human suffering has taken him beyond current evidence-based clinical treatments to an evolving and promising application of Byron Katie's The Work.

This book, *Inquiry-Based Psychotherapy: Applying The Work of Byron Katie in Clinical Settings*, invites you to actively engage in a process where you learn an approach based upon a "universal tool for self-discovery." Anil addresses the relevance of considering an integration of this approach with a variety of other clinical treatments. He provides explicit directions, tools, and articulates how this approach can be used specifically with different diagnoses along with applications for commonly experienced life difficulties. The book is grounded in clinical examples, reflection questions, and discernment for the appropriateness of the use of this approach with different diagnostic considerations. Whether a newly minted practitioner or a seasoned veteran, you can better assist clients in the self-discovery of the foundational narratives that underlie their difficulties and the inquiry that can lead to self-directed growth and change. Anil offers new ways to broaden and deepen your clinical work.

Jane Harmon Jacobs, Ph.D.
Retired Academic Dean at Antioch University Seattle
Retired Washington State Licensed Psychologist
Past President, Washington State Psychological Association

# ACKNOWLEDGEMENTS

I am deeply grateful to the many people who have supported me in writing this book.

First and foremost, I want to thank my clients, who continue to teach me so much. Your insights and experiences have been invaluable.

I could not have completed this project without the unwavering support of my family. To my wife, Arlyce, thank you for your enormous patience and understanding over the past few years as I dedicated myself to the writing process. And to my son, Arun, your motivation and gentle pressure helped keep me on track whenever I started to slack off.

I am honored to have forewords contributed by two esteemed colleagues. Dr. Deepa Rao and Dr. Jane Jacobs, thank you for lending your expertise and generous endorsements of this work. I am indebted to Dr. Janice Harper for generously serving as my writing coach and helping me hone my ideas and prose. To Ms. Lieve Maas, thank you for the stunning cover design and your meticulous work on the interior edits.

I had the great fortune of many illuminating discussions that shaped my thinking for this book. For those thought-provoking conversations, I am grateful to Mr. Stephen Mitchell, Dr. Debra

London, Dr. Ariel Ganz, Mr. Ricardo Hidalgo, Mr. David Johnston, Ms. Jackie Luff, Dr. Shahar Lev-Ari, Dr. John Moritsugu, Mr. Ken Farber, Ms. Nadine Ferris France, Ms. Grace Bell and Ms. Marie Odiel van Rhijn.

I want to express my eternal gratitude to Byron Katie for her gift of The Work to the world and her tireless efforts to end human suffering. Her wisdom and insight have been a guiding light throughout this journey.

I also want to thank my dear friend Celeste Gabriel, who introduced me to The Work and guided me through many mind-blowing insights as she facilitated my personal work. Her support and encouragement have been invaluable.

Finally, my heartfelt appreciation goes to Dr. Petia Sierschynski and Ms. Tamara Dyer for taking the time to provide a careful proofread of the manuscript. I am also indebted to the nearly one hundred psychotherapists who took the time to complete an online survey about their use of The Work of Byron Katie in their practice. Your feedback and insights were immensely helpful in shaping this book.

This book is a collaborative effort, and the support from so many humbles me. Any errors or omissions are, of course, entirely my own. Thank you all for helping bring this much-delayed project to fruition.

# TERMINOLOGY

Please note that throughout this text, I use the following terms interchangeably to refer to the same process:

a. The Work of Byron Katie
b. The Work (TW)
c. Inquiry-Based Stress Reduction (IBSR)
d. Inquiry

# TABLE OF CONTENTS

**Introduction** 1

**PART I** 7

**Chapter 1** 9

**Why Use The Work of Byron Katie in Psychotherapy?**

- Trauma and Bent Pennies 8
- The Power of Underlying Beliefs in Psychiatric Diagnosis 10
- Universal Applicability of The Work 12
- Summary 18
- Reflection Questions 19

**Chapter 2** 20

**The Power of Illusions and How Our Brains Can Be Deceived**

- The Power of Illusions: Expanding the Connection to The Work 22
- Summary 26
- Reflection Questions 27

**Chapter 3** 28

**Differences Between The Work And Other Forms Of Therapies**

- The Work and Cognitive Behavioral Therapy (CBT) 27
- The Work and Dialectical Behavioral Therapy 29
- The Work and Schema Therapy 29
- Transactional Analysis Script Theory and The Work 30
- Summary 36
- Reflection Questions 37

**PART II** 38

**Chapter 4** 40

**How To Do TW in a Clinical Setting**

How to Identify Core Stories 42

How to Help Your Client Complete the *Judge-Your-Neighbor Worksheet* 45

Summary 48

Reflection Questions 49

**Chapter 5** 51

**How To Help Your Client Move Into Inquiry Using the Four Questions**

First question: *Is it true?* 52

Second question: *Can you absolutely know that it's true?* 52

Third question: *How do you react, what happens, when you believe that thought?* 52

Fourth Question: *Who would you be without that thought?* 59

Summary 64

Reflection Questions 65

**Chapter 6** 67

**The Work as a Meditation**

Time and Mental Health 68

The Importance of Writing 69

Understanding the Three Kinds of Business 70

Summary 72

Reflection Questions 73

**PART III** 75
**Using TW with Specific Diagnosis and Clinical Situations**

**Chapter 7** 77
**Addictions**
Reflection Questions 89

**Chapter 8** 91
**Anxiety**
Reflection Questions 97

**Chapter 9** 99
**Abusive Relationships**
Reflection Questions 103

**Chapter 10** 105
**Cancer, Illness, and Disabilities**
Reflection Questions 111

**Chapter 11** 113
**Eating Disorders**
Reflection Questions 121

**Chapter 12** 123
**Procrastination and Perfectionism**
Reflection Questions 127

**Chapter 13** 129
**Suicide and Depression**
Reflection Questions 139

**Chapter 14** 141

**Prejudice**

Reflection Questions 151

**PART IV** 153

**Chapter 15** 155

**Going Deeper in The Work**

Summary 160

Reflection Questions 161

**Chapter 16** 163

**Critiques of The Work**

Re-traumatization of Patients with PTSD 163

Lack of Empirical Evidence 165

Oversimplification 165

Fear of Loss of Autonomy 167

Insufficient Focus on Emotions 168

Potential for Spiritual Bypassing 169

Lack of Formal Training 172

The Work is a Cult 173

The Transformative Power of The Work—A New Paradigm 175

Summary 178

Reflection Questions 179

**Chapter 17** 181

**The Challenges and Rewards of Doing The Work in Clinical Settings**

Summary 192

Reflection Questions 193

**Chapter 18** 195

**Research and Future Directions**

Summary 204

Reflection Questions 205

**Conclusion** 207

**The Journey Ahead**

**Bibliography** 211

# INTRODUCTION

When you first encounter The Work of Byron Katie, you might find the concepts fascinating. Perhaps you're even eager to apply them with your clients. But if you're like many therapists, this initial excitement might give way to confusion or uncertainty about how to translate these principles into actionable therapeutic interventions.

You might have some limiting beliefs or assumptions about The Work. Maybe you're concerned about its applicability to your clientele or feel it might be too abstract for your current practice. These misconceptions can hold you back from exploring its full potential.

But let's consider what The Work can genuinely offer. It's been incredibly effective for a wide range of clients, including those dealing with anxiety, depression, relationship issues, and self-esteem problems. The flexibility and depth of The Work can enhance your existing treatment approaches, adding new dimensions and perspectives.

You might still have questions or concerns, and that's where this guide comes in. I've created it to bridge the gap between your curiosity and practical application. It's designed to walk you through the principles and techniques by providing step-by-step instructions for integrating The Work of Byron Katie into your clinical practice.

Byron Katie, a bestselling author and speaker, stumbled upon the process she called The Work after experiencing a life-altering epiphany in the late 1980s. By questioning her thoughts and beliefs, she discovered a new way of perceiving reality that liberated her from emotional torment and sparked a desire to share this insight with others. The Work is a process that may seem simple but is quite powerful. It challenges our assumptions, judgments, and expectations through four questions and a radical process called turnaround, which lets you experience the opposite of the stressful thought you are believing. This process can help to remove the layers of our egoic mind and reveal the truth of our being. Millions of people around the world have used The Work to overcome various psychological and emotional issues such as self-doubt, anxiety, addiction, and relationship problems.

The Work of Byron Katie, often simply referred to as The Work, is a powerful method of self-inquiry that helps individuals identify and question the thoughts that cause their suffering. Developed by Byron Katie in the 1980s, The Work consists of four questions and a turnaround process that enables people to explore their stressful beliefs and discover a more peaceful, liberating perspective.

The four questions of The Work are:

1. Is it true?
2. Can you absolutely know that it's true?
3. How do you react, what happens, when you believe that thought?
4. Who would you be without the thought?

After answering these questions, individuals are invited to find turnarounds, which are alternative interpretations of their original thought that may be equally or more true. By engaging in this process, people can break free from the grip of their stressful thoughts and find a clearer, more compassionate understanding of themselves and others.

The Work has been used effectively to address a wide range of issues, including relationships, anxiety, depression, addictions, and more. It can be practiced independently or with the guidance of a facilitator, and has been adopted by mental health professionals worldwide as a complementary tool in psychotherapy.

***

Welcome to *Inquiry-Based Psychotherapy: Applying The Work of Byron Katie in Clinical Settings*. I've written this book for mental health professionals who want to incorporate The Work into their clinical practice but may be unsure about how to start.

I will offer a clear and evidence-based perspective on its effectiveness in clinical practice. I'll address common misunderstandings and provide scientific evidence to support its use as a therapeutic approach.

Byron Katie's first book, *Loving What Is* (Katie & Mitchell, Loving what is: four questions that can change your life, 2002), quickly became a bestseller. *Loving What Is* explores the fundamental principles of The Work and features many compelling case studies that demonstrate the effectiveness of this innovative approach to personal growth and healing.

Since the release of *Loving What Is*, Byron Katie has become a prominent figure in the fields of personal development and spirituality. Her inspiring presence and insightful teachings have encouraged countless people to start their own journey of self-discovery and transformation. She has written several other books, including the thought-provoking *A Thousand Names for Joy* (Katie & Mitchell, A thousand names for joy: living in harmony with the way things are, 2007), *I Need Your Love—Is That True?* (Katie & Katz, I need your love—is that true?: how to stop seeking love, approval, and appreciation and start finding them instead, 2005), and the groundbreaking *A Mind at Home with Itself* (Katie & Mitchell, A mind at home with itself: how asking four questions can free your mind, open your heart, and turn your world around, 2017). These works deepen our understanding of The Work and its potential impact on the human experience.

The COVID-19 pandemic has caused a seismic shift in the mental health landscape, and as psychotherapists, we are witnessing its effects (Kaiser Family Foundation, 2023). The 2021 US Surgeon General's Report of the Youth Mental Health Advisory Board confirms that anxiety, depression, and substance abuse disorders have surged across the population (US Surgeon General, 2021). The pandemic has spawned a pandemic of mental suffering due to isolation, uncertainty, and fear, threatening to overwhelm us all.

The rise in youth suicide rates is one of the most alarming trends reported by *The National Institutes of Mental Health* (National Institute of Mental Health, 2023). The pandemic has left young people feeling adrift, disconnected, and hopeless. Their sense of normalcy has shattered due to disruptions in schooling, socializing, and support systems.

The pandemic's impact has also made it difficult for clients to find therapists. The shift to telehealth has caused a sudden increase in demand for mental health services, leading to a shortage of therapists (APA, 2021). As a result, many clients are left languishing on waitlists or struggling to find help. As therapists, we must acknowledge this stark reality and find ways to expand our reach and make our services more accessible and equitable for all.

It's important to acknowledge the truth that we need to take care of ourselves just as much as we care for others. In the following chapters, I will explain how The Work can be a valuable tool to help us work more efficiently and effectively.

This book is designed to be flexible and user-friendly, so you can use it in any way that suits your needs. You can read each chapter to gain a comprehensive understanding of how to use The Work in clinical settings. Alternatively, you can jump to the chapters that resonate the most with you or address the issues you're currently dealing with.

To enhance your learning and engagement, I've included case studies that illustrate the application of The Work in real-world situations, discussion questions that prompt reflection and dialogue, and practical exercises that help you understand and apply the strategies in your work. Additionally, links to additional resources and articles provide further insights and inspiration.

To protect the privacy of my clients, I have changed identifying details such as gender, age, and specific situations. Similarities to actual individuals are purely coincidental, as all identifying characteristics have been intentionally altered.

# PART I

# CHAPTER 1

## Why Use The Work of Byron Katie in Psychotherapy?

In this chapter, you will learn about the significant impact traumatic events have on mental health, mainly stemming from the false beliefs formed in their aftermath. While psychiatric diagnosis can pinpoint symptoms, it often overlooks these deep-rooted narratives. The Work provides a method to question and reframe these beliefs, granting individuals a clearer perception of reality. As therapists, introducing The Work into our toolkit can move beyond mere coping strategies, guiding clients towards a profound liberation from their limiting beliefs.

As a therapist, do you ever feel burnt out and unsure how to support your clients? It's common to feel like you've tried everything, and nothing seems to be working. I suggest considering The Work of Byron Katie for a fresh perspective. It can also be helpful when you're struggling to find the right words to help your clients. I'll guide you through the process clearly and understandably so you can experience The Work's transformative power for yourself. But first, let me share a story with you.

Anne, a 30-year-old professional woman, had always been haunted by the memory of a trauma she had experienced when she was just five years old and had discovered her parents having intercourse. As she was trying to make sense of what she was seeing and thinking her father—an angry drunk—was hurting her mother, her dad yelled at her to go back to her room. She fled to her room, realizing she had seen something she was not supposed to see. Anne was convinced she had done something wrong and was a bad person. Her belief became reinforced when, shortly after, her mother began coming to her room at night to avoid her father. The experience had left her feeling shaken and confused, and she had never been able to discuss it with anyone.

"I came to believe that there was something wrong with me." Her voice broke, and tears rolled down her cheeks as she told me about this incident. She paused to take a tissue and dab her face, her hands shaking. She was convinced she was to blame for her parents' problems.

Anne's deep-seated belief that something was wrong with her weakened as I gently challenged that belief using The Work of Byron Katie. She could now see how holding onto this mistaken idea had been damaging her for many years. She could instead see how the opposite belief "I'm perfect just as I am"—was more accurate. Anne realized that she needed to forgive herself to move on. As we used The Work in our therapeutic sessions, she was finally able to let go of the guilt and resentment she had been carrying around for so long. Her mistaken belief was what I call her "bent penny," —and by using The Work of Byron Katie, you will learn to uncover the "bent pennies" holding your clients back from living their best possible lives.

## Trauma and Bent Pennies

During my Transactional Analysis training in London, I was introduced to the parable of the Bent Penny. The story goes that if you have a stack of pennies and a bent penny is somewhere in the stack, the lower the penny is, the more unstable the stack becomes. Anne's belief was like a bent penny low in the stack. Each subsequent traumatic event she suffered was like adding another bent coin to the pile, making it more likely to fall. Her belief that she had been a bad child became a story that she told over and over to herself, a story that became her truth.

One of the most damaging things about trauma is that it can cause us to develop distorted beliefs about ourselves. These beliefs are what Byron Katie calls our story. Most people go through life with an overarching false perception of themselves that shapes their experience of the world and can lead to a great deal of suffering.

The Work of Byron Katie offers a way to challenge these harmful beliefs and storylines. As clients explore their beliefs with The Work, they often find that they are not as accurate or valid as they first thought. This can lead to newfound clarity and peace of mind.

Byron Katie's Work is based on the principle that self-inquiry—asking questions and waiting for the answers to appear from within—can help us find peace in life. She asks us to question our thoughts and beliefs about ourselves, other people, and the world that we find stressful. Through this questioning, she has discovered that suffering comes from believing our *thoughts* about reality instead of seeing them for what they are: stories we tell ourselves.

The telling of this core story about ourselves starts in the first years of our life. Our childhood experiences and relationships reinforce this story. The core story becomes the inner blueprint we carry around. The core story becomes our identity.

We also project our story outward onto others, creating a self-reflection and helping us to enhance and maintain our story as we grow up to be adults.

Most people I have met, especially in professional settings where success is demanded, have functioned through a high-wire core story. Their act balances the belief, "I am not good enough," with its mirror image, "I am special." My clients, my colleagues, and even I sway back and forth between these two core stories.

Commanded by whom we believe ourselves to be, we manifest ourselves in this world. The outside world and the people in it are then viewed through this filter of our core story; the so-called objective world, physical and human, is tainted by our filters. In other words, our beliefs create our life experiences. These beliefs, therefore, are at the root of all mental illness and unhappiness in this world.

I am not suggesting that we must eliminate all our beliefs. I am not sure that is even possible. However, it is essential to recognize those beliefs that hold us back in our lives and relationships. By natural extension, thoughts play a significant role in the psychopathology of mental illness. I have often heard Katie say: "I don't let go of my stressful thoughts. I question *them,* and they let go of *me.*

## The Power of Underlying Beliefs in Psychiatric Diagnosis

Let us consider some examples of certain beliefs in psychiatric diagnoses.

According to the Diagnostic and Statistical Manual of Mental Disorders 5$^{th}$ Edition (DSM-V-TR), the diagnostic criteria for depression include "feelings of worthlessness or excessive or inappropriate guilt nearly every day."

In my years of working with clients under the sway of major depressive disorders, I consistently hear a belief in their worthlessness, even from clients who are high achievers. They tend to exaggerate their feelings of worthlessness, which may reach delusional levels. If a client's depression is part of a bipolar disorder, during a manic episode, they may host a belief at the opposite end of the spectrum: an inflated sense of importance or grandiosity.

One of the most common reasons clients see a psychotherapist is to treat anxiety disorders. Anxiety is caused when we project our beliefs onto an imagined future, spinning all kinds of possible adverse scenarios in our minds and experiencing stress over these imagined futures. In the case of adults, they might worry about job responsibilities. Children may dread performing in school. These imagined futures can be summed up with the acronym FEAR: False Evidence Appearing Real. As Katie says, "If you want to be afraid, get a future."

For example, people with obsessive-compulsive disorder (OCD) have anxiety characterized by constant, irrational **beliefs about dirt, germs, or contamination**. They may also harbor **excessive concerns about accidentally or purposefully injuring another person**.

Yet another variant of anxiety is called phobia, wherein a person suffers an intense fear of some object or situation. An example is a person convinced beyond doubt that a **spider will kill them**. In reality, we know this is a distorted belief that very few species of spiders are poisonous to the potency to be able to kill a human being.

The National Health Service hospital where I worked in North London specialized in treating anorexia nervosa. This eating disorder is experienced as an intense fear of gaining weight or becoming fat, even though the person may be grossly underweight. I have noticed that even people who are significantly underweight, to the point of needing intravenous feeding, have a robust and **distorted belief that they are overweight or obese**. Their core story may have them convinced that even **eating a banana or an apple would make them gain excessive weight**.

Post-traumatic stress disorder (PTSD) is another anxiety-related condition caused by an adverse reaction to a traumatic or highly stressful event. Many inhumane victimizations, including war, physical or sexual abuse, and violent crime, can bring it out. Those with PTSD experience persistent and exaggerated negative beliefs or expectations about themselves, others, or the world: "I

**am bad." "I can trust no one." Or "The world is perilous."** While these fears do stem from suffering actual traumatic experiences in the past, PTSD forces people to develop irrational beliefs that similar traumas must recur in the future.

Strong, distorted beliefs are also at the root of many of the most severe mental disorders, such as schizophrenia, wherein delusions and hallucinations assault people internally to the point that they cannot differentiate between fantasy and reality. People with **paranoid schizophrenia are often hyper-preoccupied with one or more delusional beliefs**: they smell odors or hear sounds that others cannot; they detect malevolent intent in certain people's innocent behaviors. This psychosis can seriously impair the quality of life to the point of utter immobility. The Work cannot "cure" psychosis but can help someone suffering from debilitating negative beliefs begin to see a perspective not limited by their constraining beliefs.

By helping your client identify the limiting belief(s) and guiding them to see the toll it takes on their emotional life and relationships with themselves and others, The Work is especially effective in helping clients challenge these core stories and see how the turnarounds are as true as or more accurate than, their closely held beliefs. Using the turnarounds empowers your clients and gives them a tool for life. The materials for doing The Work are also free and easy to use. You'll find that using The Work in your practice is practical, fast, and functions in the here and now without unnecessarily digging into your client's past—something that necessitates long-term analysis while your client continues to struggle with maladaptive thoughts or behavioral patterns.

## Universal Applicability of The Work

As therapists, it's essential to acknowledge and honor the diversity each client brings to the therapeutic space. When working with clients from different cultures, it's crucial to consider the various aspects of their identity, such as race, ethnicity, gender, sexual orientation, socioeconomic status, and culture.

The Work, which involves a set of core questions that can be applied in any context, can be a powerful tool for exploring thoughts and beliefs. However, cultural competence is essential to use it effectively with clients from diverse backgrounds.

Embracing cultural competence in our practice is necessary and a pathway to success. It means adapting our methods to meet clients' unique needs creating a therapeutic space where they feel valued and heard. It also requires us to examine our own biases and assumptions, continuously educate ourselves, and reflect on our practice. This commitment enriches our clients' lives and helps us evolve as therapists, leading to more effective and fulfilling therapeutic outcomes.

Working with clients from diverse backgrounds may present challenges, such as language barriers and different expressions of distress. However, these challenges are not obstacles but stepping stones for growth and learning. They provide unique opportunities for the therapist and the client to broaden their understanding, deepen their empathy, and enhance their therapeutic journey.

By delving into case studies and testimonials, we can witness the transformative power of The Work across a diverse range of identities. When applied with cultural competence, this approach enriches our clients' lives and propels us forward as therapists. It opens doors to new perspectives, fosters deeper connections, and paves the way for more effective therapeutic interventions.

Ultimately, our commitment to cultural competence reflects our dedication to creating a more inclusive and effective therapeutic environment that honors the diversity of human experience.

Many people think we cannot control our beliefs, much less help our clients change theirs. That is simply untrue. Most children in the West believe in Santa Claus or the tooth fairy. However, as adults, we no longer believe in Santa Claus and the tooth fairy. We did not have to put out any effort or do any technique to get rid of those beliefs. This is perhaps a light-hearted example, yet it points out that beliefs can transform with growth and understanding.

There is an ancient Buddhist metaphor: "It's not a snake; it's a rope." Imagine yourself walking with a friend in an area that rattlesnakes inhabit. You are walking at dusk, and the light is low. You come around a corner and spot a curvy, 6-foot-long object in front of you. Most likely, your body will react in fear, thinking the curved line is a snake. Your sympathetic system will prepare your body to fight, flee, or freeze. Your friend might shine a flashlight on "the snake." With great relief, you then realize that somebody had dropped a piece of rope on the path!

Fear dissipates when the individual sees that what they feared is just a rope, not a snake. This example illustrates how beliefs and fears rather than reality can influence the body's response. Once the misconception is removed, the mind shift causes a transformation in the body.

One of my main goals in writing *Applying The Work of Byron Katie in Clinical Settings* is to demonstrate how all the main events in life happen *to* us. We do not control life as we believe in our core stories. We do not choose to be born, when, or where to be born. We do not get to choose our parents or social status. At birth, we do not choose the sex, skin color, or nationality we are born with. We do not get to decide how or when we die either. So, could it be a delusion that we get to decide on everything between birth and death?

I realize this is a highly controversial statement, and many of you will be incensed to hear my suggestion that we have no choice.

Yet, please reserve judgment until you've read the following pages, for I will show you that there are many things in life we feel had come to us of our free will when, in fact, options were never there in the first place.

As professionals using The Work, you will find that it can keep you clear-headed, prevent burnout, and give you hope when you would otherwise feel cynical or despairing about helping your clients get better. Incorporating The Work of Byron Katie into your practice can serve as a vital safeguard against professional burnout in many ways. For one, the methodology demands that you, too, question your own beliefs and assumptions, keeping your mental landscape fresh and agile. This self-inquiry can serve as a form of self-care, helping you avoid the staleness that can lead to burnout. More than that, facilitating your clients through The Work can offer you a sense of renewed purpose. As you guide them through their transformative process, you'll witness firsthand the positive impact of your facilitation. This can bring about a more profound sense of gratification and achievement in your work, acting as a wellspring of emotional resilience. Engaging in The Work can renew your professional vitality, making your practice a place for your clients to find peace and a sanctuary for your own well-being.

## SUMMARY

- Traumatic events and distorted beliefs contribute to mental instability and suffering over time, shaping core stories that become inner blueprints and identities.
- Core stories are influential in the psychopathology of mental illnesses, such as depression and anxiety disorders, but The Work assists clients in recognizing and challenging limiting beliefs, leading to clarity and peace of mind.
- Anxiety arises from projecting beliefs onto an imagined future, creating false evidence appearing real (FEAR). The Work helps clients identify and challenge distorted beliefs and core stories, addressing the root of severe mental disorders.
- The turnarounds empower clients and provide a lifelong tool while life events are beyond our control, occurring between birth and death.

## REFLECTION QUESTIONS

1. As you read about Anne's experience, what thoughts or feelings come up for you about past clients you've worked with who held deep-seated beliefs from childhood trauma? How might The Work have been helpful for them?

2. Do you notice any "bent pennies" in your clients? How might you gently begin to explore these beliefs with The Work?

3. The chapter discusses how anxiety disorders are often caused by projecting fearful beliefs onto an imagined future. Can you recall a client who struggled with this? What might that look like if you were to guide them through questioning their anxious thoughts?

4. How do you typically feel when you've tried many interventions with a client, but nothing seems to help shift their suffering? What potential do you see for The Work to bring a fresh perspective in these situations?

5. Did any part of the explanation about how beliefs create our life experiences resonate with your views? How might you explain this idea to a skeptical client?

# CHAPTER 2

## The Power of Illusions and How Our Brains Can Be Deceived

Do you struggle to help clients who jump to negative conclusions? Have you ever had a client like Emily, a 40-year-old woman plagued by social anxiety, who instantly interprets others' facial expressions or tones of voice as signs of disapproval or rejection? She avoids social events and is convinced that people are judging her negatively. Emily's past experiences of rejection shape her current interpretations of sensory inputs, such as facial expressions or tone of voice. How do you help clients caught in this loop of negative inference, where subjective perception distorts their reality and reinforces maladaptive behaviors?

Let's start by acknowledging a fundamental truth: Our perception of reality does not perfectly mirror objective truth. Instead, it is a subjective construct shaped by our brains' interpretation of sensory inputs. Confined within the walls of our skulls, our brains cannot directly know the external world. They must infer the causes behind the sensory effects they receive—a phenomenon known as the reverse inference problem. The "reverse inference problem" in cognitive neuroscience refers to the logical issue of inferring specific mental states or cognitive processes from brain activation patterns observed in neuroimaging studies, such as fMRI. This inference is termed "reverse" because it moves from data (brain activation) to hypothesis (cognitive state), which is the opposite direction of traditional deductive reasoning. However, this ability for internal creation can sometimes overshadow external sensory stimuli, making it harder to stay anchored in the present moment.

In this chapter, we look at instances where visual and tactile stimuli have the power to trick our brains and deceive our perception. These illusions are compelling examples that showcase how our perception can easily be manipulated, highlighting the vital significance of questioning our beliefs. By engaging with such illusions, we can gain insights into the malleability of perception and develop a better understanding of the importance of challenging our distorted beliefs. By using The Work to identify and question perceptual illusions, we can help our clients uncover and confront the distorted beliefs they may hold, facilitating personal growth and development.

The Muller-Lyer illusion is one of the best-known optical illusions (Erlebacher, 1969). It consists of two parallel lines with arrowheads pointing inwards or outwards. The illusion is created by the differing directions of the arrowheads, which trick the brain into perceiving the lines as being of different lengths. This illusion was first described by Franz Mueller-Lyer in 1889 and has been extensively studied by psychologists and neurologists. Although the illusion is well understood, its exact mechanism is still debatable. One theory suggests that the brain uses previous experience to estimate the size of objects, and the arrowheads disrupt this process. Another theory suggests that the illusion occurs because the brain interprets the direction of the arrowheads as meaning that the lines are receding or approaching. Regardless of its exact cause, the Muller-Lyer illusion is a fascinating example of how simple visual cues can fool our brains.

Another example demonstrating how visual and tactile stimuli can fool our brains is the "rubber hand illusion." (Ramakonar, 2011) In this test, healthy participants sat at a table with their forearms and right hand hidden behind a curtain. A lifelike rubber hand was placed in front of them, lined up with their right shoulder.

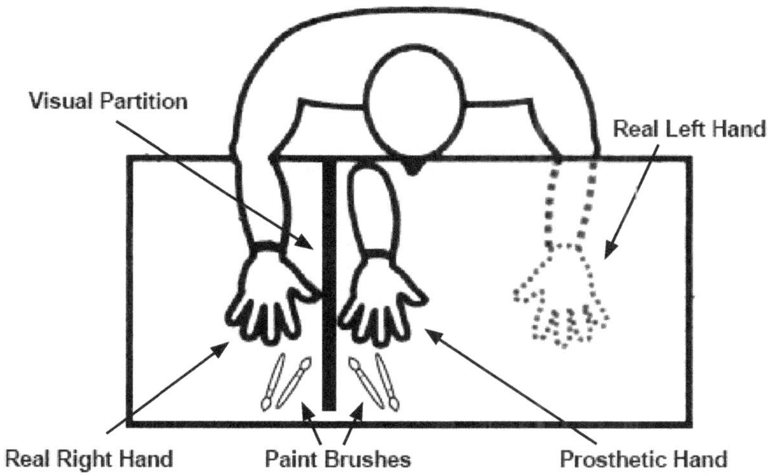


The deception sets in when the real and fake hands are stroked simultaneously and quickly for a minute or two. When combined, the brain confuses the visual information with the tactile sensations. When asked to describe their feelings, volunteers stated that it appeared as if their own hands had vanished while their fake hands had become theirs. When the phony palm is hit with a hammer, the participant's real hand is scooped up in surprise. This experiment implies that our brains may be fooled into believing we are feeling things we are not actually experiencing. This can be valuable information for understanding how our brain works and how it can be fooled. Let us explore how these concepts help to show how The Work approaches perception and how to alter our perceptions toward more constructive ends.

## The Power of Illusions: Expanding the Connection to The Work

The Muller-Lyer and rubber hand illusions exemplify how our brains can be deceived by visual and tactile stimuli, demonstrating that perceptions can be altered. This concept is central to The Work, which is a process of self-inquiry that encourages questioning our perspectives. In this analysis, we will examine the relationship between these illusions and The Work and their relevance in therapeutic settings.

The Work assists individuals in identifying and scrutinizing stories they create in their minds, determining if they are based in reality or simply in distorted perceptions. The illusions mentioned above serve as metaphors for distorted beliefs about oneself, others, or the world. For instance, someone might perceive themselves as unworthy of love or as a failure based on interpretations of visual cues, much like the Muller-Lyer illusion, which creates false perceptions of line lengths. The Work encourages questioning the validity of such beliefs and considering alternative perspectives.

In therapy, the power of illusion can be utilized to help clients comprehend distorted perceptions and their impact on mental well-being. By presenting the Muller-Lyer and rubber hand illusions, therapists can demonstrate our susceptibility to deception and the potential inaccuracy of thoughts and beliefs. Incorporating illusions in therapy sessions provides a compelling visual and experiential aid, highlighting the significance of questioning assumptions and examining thought patterns.

Illusions serve as powerful metaphors for the mental constructs that often imprison us and our clients. Like Emily, your clients may be entrapped by their cognitive illusions, interpreting sensory inputs through a distorted lens shaped by past experiences and subjective assumptions. These illusions, whether they pertain to social interactions, self-worth, or even body image, can significantly impair their quality of life and mental well-being. These are not much different from optical illusions that trick the eye; they are mental illusions that deceive the mind.

The Work is a systematic process of inquiry that helps individuals question the beliefs and assumptions fueling their illusions. Imagine helping Emily—or clients like her—through The Work's four questions and turnarounds. You guide them to question the validity of their thoughts ("Is it true that the person disapproves of me?"), explore the emotional repercussions of their beliefs ("How do I react when I believe that thought?"), and consider alternative realities ("Who would I be without that thought?"). As they engage in this rigorous self-inquiry, they begin to dismantle the illusions that have long held them captive. The Work offers a systematic way to break down these mental constructs, allowing your clients to see the world—and themselves—in a more objective and compassionate light.

## SUMMARY

- The rubber hand illusion demonstrates how the brain can confuse visual and tactile stimuli and be fooled into believing it is feeling something it is not.
- In therapeutic settings, the power of illusion can be utilized to help your clients comprehend distorted perceptions and their impact on mental well-being. You can present these illusions as compelling visual and experiential aids, highlighting the significance of questioning beliefs and examining thought patterns.
- By using The Work to identify and question perceptual illusions, you can facilitate personal growth and development in your clients.

# REFLECTION QUESTIONS

1. How might you use the concepts of optical and tactile illusions like the Muller-Lyer and rubber hand illusions to help clients understand cognitive distortions? What are some ways to incorporate them into sessions?

2. When has a client had a firmly held belief or perception that turned out to be distorted or inaccurate? How did questioning their belief using inquiry help reveal the distortion?

3. What deeply rooted stories or perceptions do you tend to hold about yourself as a therapist? How could you apply the principles of The Work to investigate and challenge these views?

4. How might the realization that our minds can deceive us pave the way for self-inquiry? In your experience, what makes people more open to questioning their thoughts and beliefs?

5. How has your understanding of perception, illusion, and cognitive distortion evolved through learning about The Work? What new insights has this chapter provided, and how might it shape your approach with clients?

# CHAPTER 3

## Differences Between The Work And Other Forms Of Therapies

In this chapter, we will explore the similarities and differences between Cognitive Behavioral Therapy (CBT) and The Work. Additionally, we will delve into the relationship between The Work and Dialectical Behavioral Therapy (DBT). Furthermore, I compare Schema Therapy and The Work. Lastly, I compare Transactional Analysis's Script Theory and The Work.

### The Work and Cognitive Behavioral Therapy (CBT)

Both CBT and The Work share some common features, such as a focus on identifying and challenging self-defeating beliefs. However, there are also some key differences between the two approaches. For instance, CBT typically involves longer-term therapy sessions with a trained therapist, while The Work can be done independently with or without a facilitator. CBT tends to be more directive, with the therapist providing guidance and feedback during sessions.

In contrast, The Work is based on the premise that everyone can find their own answers. As a result, sessions tend to be shorter and more focused on inquiry and self-exploration. Despite these differences, CBT and The Work can be effective in helping individuals overcome negative thinking patterns and achieve lasting change.

However, a few key differences exist between The Work of Byron Katie and CBT. My colleague and fellow psychotherapist in the

Bay Area, Ken Farber, distinguishes between Deliberative Thinking and Witnessing Awareness/Receptive Attention. Deliberative thinking occurs when one is consciously and intentionally thinking about something (Farber, 2007). With deliberative thinking, one experiences oneself as doing one's thinking. Witnessing awareness occurs when one asks the question and observes what arises in awareness in response to the question. There is no attempt to control thoughts or intellectually analyze what is arising in awareness in response to the questions. Cultivating this witnessing awareness is the core process involved in the inquiry process. Therefore, in inquiry, there are no right or wrong answers. So, in The Work, after a question is asked, your client is instructed to listen internally with a witnessing awareness and wait to see if an answer arises from within to meet the question. CBT, on the other hand, uses deliberative thinking to answer questions. In practice, for most people, doing The Work would involve a mix of deliberative thinking and witnessing awareness in the beginning. Another critical difference between the two is a felt shift in the body when there is a therapeutic change. In my experience, people who experience this somatic shift tend to stick with the practice of inquiry more than those who do not.

In CBT, the client is taught to replace negative thoughts with positive thoughts, while in The Work, it is all about awareness of thoughts. In other words, The Work is about understanding the role of thoughts rather than disputing or manipulating thoughts—very similar to the approaches in Acceptance and Commitment Therapy (ACT) and Mindfulness-Based Cognitive Therapy (MBCT). Change occurs naturally through the process of witnessing the effects of one's thinking. Thereby, your clients begin to derive a sense of self separate from the content of their thoughts. The fourth question of The Work—"Who would you be without that thought?" invites your client to step into that space of witnessing awareness.

## The Work and Dialectical Behavioral Therapy

In Dialectical Behavioral Therapy (DBT), the concept of the "wise mind" refers to a state of mind in which an individual is able to integrate and balance their emotional and rational minds. It is a state of being where one can access one's intuitive, emotional, and intellectual abilities to make decisions and navigate difficult situations.

The idea behind the "wise mind" is that when we are emotionally distressed, we tend to be in a state of emotional mind, where we react impulsively and based on our emotions without considering the facts or consequences of our actions. On the other hand, when we are in a purely rational state of mind, we may be disconnected from our emotions and fail to take them into account when making decisions.

The "wise mind" is the middle ground between these two states, where emotions and reason are integrated to form a balanced approach to decision-making. It is a state of mind where one is able to use both their emotional and rational capacities to make effective decisions and navigate challenging situations.

In DBT, therapists help clients access their "wise mind" state by teaching various skills, including mindfulness, emotion regulation, distress tolerance, and interpersonal effectiveness. By learning to access this state of mind, clients can improve their ability to manage difficult emotions, make effective decisions, and navigate challenging situations.

## The Work and Schema Therapy

Schema therapy is a relatively new integrative approach to psychotherapy that is effective in treating various psychological problems. It combines elements from cognitive behavioral therapy, attachment and object relations theories, and Gestalt and experiential therapies. Schema therapy is based on the idea that our early life experiences can shape how we think, feel, and behave in adulthood. The goal of Schema Therapy is to help clients become aware of their schemas (patterns of thinking, feeling, and behaving) and learn how to modify them to improve their quality of life. Schema therapy focuses on developing a healthy sense of self and repairing damaged self-esteem.

In Schema Therapy, the role of self-image is essential in changing negative patterns of thought and behavior. Schema therapists help patients identify their self-image or how they see themselves and then work to change it. This can be done by assisting patients to become aware of their schemas and how they impact their lives. Patients then work to change their self-image by challenging their schemas and developing new, more positive ways of thinking about themselves.

However, rather than focusing on changing the self-image, The Work of Byron Katie helps individuals examine their beliefs about themselves, others, and the world around them. This is done through self-inquiry, in which individuals question their thoughts and beliefs. The Work invites clients to see themselves, others, and the world without the filter of self-limiting beliefs. As your clients become more adept at cultivating witnessing awareness, they begin to grow in equanimity.

### Transactional Analysis Script Theory and The Work

Transactional Analysis (TA), created by Dr. Eric Berne, delves into the idea of "life scripts." These unconscious patterns and behaviors rooted in childhood shape an individual's decisions and relationships throughout life. Stemming from early parental messages and experiences, these scripts often lead to repetitive, sometimes limiting, or dysfunctional patterns. In TA, therapists collaborate with clients to uncover, comprehend, and strategize ways to modify these scripts. This fosters self-awareness and empowers individuals to align decisions with their true selves.

Scripts People Live is a pivotal work by Claude Steiner, a renowned expert in Transactional Analysis. The book deepens our understanding of life scripts, building on Eric Berne's foundational thoughts. Steiner presents life scripts as unconscious blueprints steering our behaviors, choices, and interpersonal dynamics. Crafted in early childhood and influenced by parental interactions and societal cues, these scripts can empower or hinder us, setting paths towards success, adversity, contentment, or despair.

Steiner introduced "script cure"—a therapeutic intervention aimed at identifying, grasping, and remolding life scripts. This method demands a profound therapist-client bond, guiding clients to unearth their script, challenge its premises, and craft a more genuine life roadmap.

Though both TA's script theory and Katie's core story address the foundational narratives steering our lives, their methods differ in their approaches to transforming limiting unconscious patterns.

A key distinction is that TA relies more heavily on the therapist-client relationship as an avenue for uncovering and reshaping life scripts. The therapy process aims to foster trust, rapport, and depth in the relationship, which becomes a vessel for exploring the genesis and evolution of scripts. The Work, in contrast, emphasizes self-inquiry as the primary vehicle for transformation. While support and guidance from a facilitator can be valuable, the inner questioning process is the primary driver of change.

TA often involves a more extensive process of exploring one's past, unconscious motivations, and the broader emotional landscape. The Work primarily focuses on questioning thoughts and beliefs in the present moment. While some context can be helpful, excessive digging into the past is seen as distracting from the core work of inquiry.

Additionally, TA utilizes the relationship with the therapist as a form of corrective experience for transforming limiting scripts. In contrast, The Work does not rely on the facilitator relationship as the healing agent per se. The inner work of questioning thoughts is viewed as the active ingredient, with the facilitator merely guiding the process.

Having delved deep into The Work's unique aspects and comparisons with other therapeutic modalities, you might wonder about its limitations and criticisms. As with any therapeutic approach, The Work is not without its critics. In a later chapter, we will explore the various critiques, shedding light on concerns and addressing potential misconceptions. From the potential risks associated with trauma to the nuances of implementing The Work in clinical practice, join me as we navigate the intricacies and address the challenges head-on.

## SUMMARY

- CBT is more directive, while The Work is based on finding your own answers through inquiry.
- The Work cultivates witnessing awareness, while CBT uses deliberative thinking.
- The Work focuses on unraveling the illusions generated by our thoughts, whereas CBT aims to substitute negative thoughts with more positive ones.
- The fourth question in The Work, which asks, "Who would you be without the thought?" shares similarities with the concept of the "wise mind" in Dialectical Behavior Therapy (DBT). Both approaches encourage a form of introspection that seeks to harmonize emotional and rational thought processes, guiding your client toward a balanced and insightful perspective.
- The goal of Schema Therapy is to develop a healthy sense of self.
- TA's Script Theory and the core story of The Work may appear similar on paper but the approaches they take clinically are very different.

# REFLECTION QUESTIONS

1. How might you explain the differences between deliberative thinking and witnessing awareness to a client new to The Work? What examples could you provide to illustrate the distinction?

2. What are the key benefits and limitations of The Work compared to more traditional talk therapies? How would you convey these to clients?

3. How might you cultivate witnessing awareness and equanimity in your clients during The Work sessions? What specific techniques could you employ?

4. How might The Work's emphasis on self-inquiry rather than changing self-image affect your work with clients' schemas and self-esteem issues? How could this be explained to clients effectively?

# PART II

# CHAPTER 4

## How To Do TW in a Clinical Setting

In this chapter, we will learn how to identify your clients' core stories and how to help them complete the Judge-Your-Neighbor Worksheet.

One of the challenges clinicians often face is how to use The Work with their clients. They have found it helpful in their own lives, but when they try to use it with clients, they get stuck. As a therapist, I'm always on the lookout for my clients' core stories, even if they don't explicitly ask for The Work. These stories are like the roots of a tree, deeply ingrained in their psyche and causing all sorts of havoc in their lives. Sometimes, it feels like we're playing a game of whack-a-mole, trying to address each individual symptom or behavior as it pops up when we should be targeting the source of the problem. And that source is often a deeply ingrained belief about themselves or others. Eric Berne called them "Scripts" in Transactional Analysis Psychotherapy, and boy, are they powerful! But here's the thing—by helping our clients to identify and challenge these core stories early on, we can expedite the healing process and create lasting change. It's like pulling out the weed at the root rather than just chopping off the leaves. So even if my clients don't come in asking for The Work, I'm always listening for those core stories, ready to help them uproot and replace them with something more empowering—clarity and peace.

## How to Identify Core Stories

During the intake session, I listen closely to my client's stories about their stressful situations and the important people in their lives to understand them and their experiences better. These core stories often include beliefs that cause significant stress and anxiety, such as "my boss doesn't appreciate my hard work" or "my children only contact me when they need something."

Once you have identified your clients' core stories, it is essential to actively listen for signs that indicate a belief system that can be challenged. These signs can include words like "should," "must," and "have to," which indicate that a client is adhering to a strict set of rules and expectations. Additionally, you could look for words like "always" and "never," which may be signs that a client is thinking in absolutes and not allowing for any exceptions.

Once these beliefs have been identified, you can use The Work to help your clients question and challenge them. Through careful inquiry, you can help your clients see their situations in a new light and develop more constructive beliefs that support their emotional well-being. Questions like "What would happen if I let go of this belief?" or "What are the effects of holding onto this belief?" can help clients gain a deeper understanding of their thought processes.

It is important to remember that identifying and challenging core stories is an ongoing process. You must continue to actively listen for signs of stressful thought patterns while also helping your clients move toward more constructive beliefs. You can help your clients create meaningful change in their lives with patience and persistence.

We will discuss two other approaches for identifying and questioning the sources of your clients' distress. Recall that we considered how cognitive behavioral therapy differs from The Work. The Work is a process of inquiry where we ask questions and wait for answers to arise from within. Even though, on the surface, it appears to be a cognitive process, it is not. Getting your client to slow down and reflect on the questions rather than answer intellectually is essential. There are no ***expected*** or ***correct*** answers. You can help this process by getting your client to imagine the scenario they are doing The Work on as vividly as possible—as if they are right there in time.

The first and straightforward method is to listen carefully to what your client is concerned or complaining about and why, because embedded in the complaint may be a belief that is causing them pain and suffering. Here is an illustrative case.

Charisse, a 28-year-old secretary, came to me last year, and right off the bat, she started complaining about the rainy weather in Seattle. She said she had been forced to move here three years ago from Arizona because her boyfriend got a lucrative offer from a big tech company. She had to say goodbye to her friends and family, and they arrived in Seattle during the fall. As you may know, Seattle has many more cloudy and drizzly days than other U.S. cities. Charisse hated the dark, wet days. She had no support besides her boyfriend, who was excited to join his new company and get a good-paying job. But the story was different for Charisse, who spent her days alone with her cat. She became depressed as the dreary Seattle weather persisted for months. As she began complaining bitterly about the Seattle weather, I invited her to complete the statement—"I complain about the Seattle weather because ……." She burst out in tears—"Because I am going to get severely depressed again."

I used this statement to guide her through the four questions and the turnarounds. When we came to the turnaround, "I am not going to get severely depressed again," a statement that could be equally valid, she became visibly more at ease as she came up with real-life examples for that turnarounds. Soon, she could see the price she paid for holding onto the belief that the weather would make her more depressed and that the opposite could be equally valid.

So here are some other examples for the prompt: I complain about ......... because .........

1. I complain about my boss because he is not interested in helping me advance in my career.
2. I complain about the grocery store clerk because she isn't trying hard to please the customers.
3. I complain about the increasing crime rate in my neighborhood because the elected officials are stuck in their political doctrines.

The "I complain about" prompt can be used to identify the underlying stressful beliefs about people or situations. However, if your client is having a particularly tough time with a person or situation, completing a Judge-Your-Neighbor Worksheet might be more beneficial. Your client begins the Worksheet by writing down any situation from their life—past, present, or future—that bothers or concerns them, whether it is about a person they dislike or worry about, someone they are angry with or frightened or saddened by, or someone they are ambivalent or puzzled about. They are invited to express their thoughts as they believe them using simple, straightforward phrases. In the initial stages of introducing The Work, it is crucial not to have your client judge themselves on the Worksheet. This is because 1) we tend to project unacceptable aspects of ourselves onto others, and 2) it is easier to learn how to turn the statements around when we write the JYN Worksheet on others.

## How to Help Your Client Complete the Judge-Your-Neighbor Worksheet

Let us go through the six questions of the Worksheet one by one:

1. In this situation, who angers, confuses, hurts, saddens, or disappoints you, and why?

   I am ...................... with ......................... because ........................

It is helpful to have your client think about a specific situation and, if possible, answer the questions as if they are with the person or in the situation in real time. It is also important to be honest and uncensored about how your client felt in that situation. Allow your client to express their feelings without any fear of judgment. Help your client to narrow down and identify precisely what upsets them in that situation or about the person they have a conflict with.

2. In this situation, how do you want them to change? What do you want them to do?

   I want .............................. to .........................

For this question, I suggest your client imagine that they are like a young child having a tantrum. Young children, when they're angry, do not censor their thoughts and are very direct in asking for what they want.

3. In this situation, what advice would you offer them? "He/she should/shouldn't ..."

I usually ask my clients to imagine they are older and wiser than the person in this situation. What advice would they offer them from their wise mind? It would be helpful for the recommendation to be precise and practical. A wise person would give advice that they know the other person would be able to do.

4. In order for you to be happy in this situation, what do you need them to think about, say, feel, or do?

   I need .................... to ...............

Most people are temporarily happy when their immediate needs are met. So this fourth question is about your client—what would bring them happiness at that moment, in that situation? Like the question above, the answers need to be specific and practical.

5. What do you think of them in this situation? Make a list. (It's okay to be petty and judgmental.)

   ............... is ................................................

We are usually taught not to judge, yet we always do it. It is essential for your client to answer this question truthfully. It is best to use single-word adjectives that describe the person.

6. What is it about this person and situation that you don't ever want to experience again?

   I don't ever want ..........................................

Your client is asked to describe the most dreaded outcome in this situation or the person with whom they have the conflict. What do they fear the most? Many clients are scared to answer this question and may need some help.

## SUMMARY

- Listen intently during intake sessions to discern core stories causing stress and anxiety in clients.
- Notice words like "should," "must," and "always," as they often hint at rigid belief systems.
- Utilize The Work to challenge these beliefs, prompting clients to reflect deeply on their thoughts.
- Maintain vigilance for recurring stressful thought patterns, guiding clients towards clarity and understanding.
- When clients voice complaints, help them articulate statements like "I complain about ..... because ....." to reveal underlying beliefs.
- Walk clients through the "Judge-Your-Neighbor Worksheet," focusing on interpersonal concerns.

# REFLECTION QUESTIONS

1. When reading this chapter, which core belief or "story" of your own came to mind? What was your internal reaction as you reflected on this belief?

2. How might actively listening for and questioning core stories enrich your work with clients? In what ways could this process expedite healing and create lasting change?

3. What fears or hesitations do you notice in yourself around inviting clients to question their core narratives? How might you work with these fears compassionately?

4. As you read the examples of identifying core stories through complaints or the Judge-Your-Neighbor Worksheet, did any client situations come to mind where you could implement this process?

5. How might you introduce elements of self-inquiry and questioning core narratives in a gradual, gentle way to clients who seem resistant? What benefits might they gain from this approach if applied with care?

# CHAPTER 5

## How To Help Your Client Move Into Inquiry Using the Four Questions

In this chapter, we'll delve deeper into the four inquiry questions and discover how to apply the Thinking→Feeling→Behavior→Outcome sequence to assist your client in a therapeutic context.

After your client has completed the Judge-Your-Neighbor Worksheet or come up with a statement to do The Work on, the next step is to help your client move into inquiry using the four questions. It is advisable to be very gentle with this process of questioning. This is not an inquisition. It would also be beneficial to give an overview of what will happen to your client.

Many years ago, a friend of mine who is a professor in the department of psychology invited me to present The Work to the psychology graduate students. I was new to The Work then, and in my enthusiasm, I did not explain The Worksheet or the four questions to the graduate students. I invited them to be very petty and judgmental as they wrote the Judge-Your-Neighbor Worksheet, and when it came to asking the first two questions and the turnarounds, a couple of the students felt I had tricked them. Hence, giving your client an overview of the four questions before the inquiry is helpful.

## First question:
## *Is it true?*

This question can, at times, stimulate the rational mind into overdrive. Instead, allow the racing thoughts to slow down and see if a single yes or no answer emerges. The only possible answers are yes or no. Any effort by your client to explain will immediately draw them out of the inquiry into mental activity. They are instructed to watch as our learned tendency to justify or qualify the answer emerges as a response to these questions.

## Second question:
## *Can you absolutely know that it's true?*

It is necessary to ask the second question only if your client answers "yes" to the first question. The second question is not an invitation to collect evidence. It is a prompt to dive deeper into inquiry to get still and wait for the answer to emerge. It does not matter if the answer is yes or no; it is OK to sit for a while with the experience of not knowing.

When I was little, my dad hit me with a stick. So, if I had written a statement, "I am angry with my dad because he hit me with a stick," my answer to the first two questions might be yes and yes. However, whatever beliefs I hold on to for years after the beating could be the real reason for my suffering. In another chapter, we will explore how to proceed when working with a factual statement.

## Third question:
## *How do you react, what happens, when you believe that thought?*

To help your client answer this question, I like to use what Katie calls the order of creation diagram.

## ORDER OF CREATION 1

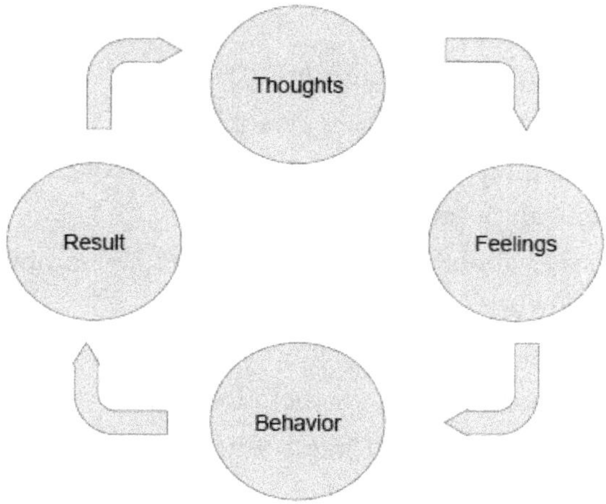


## ORDER OF CREATION 2

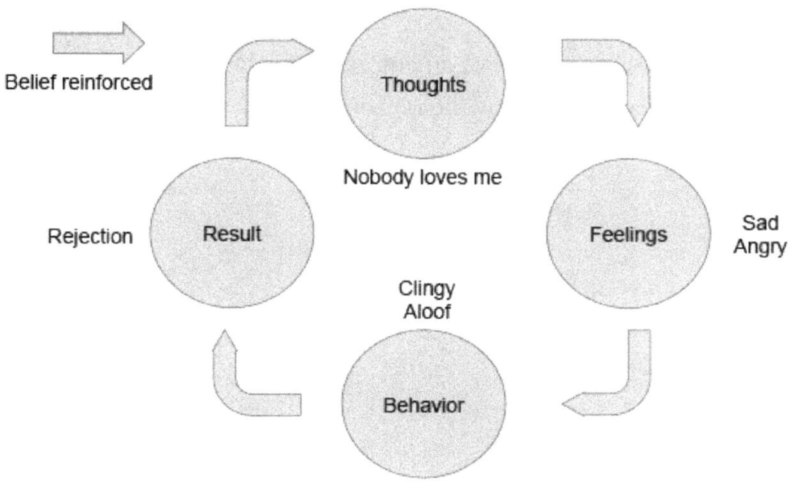

It is helpful for your client and you to consider these four prompts as they contemplate the stressful situation.

### *Thoughts*

What thoughts or images come up?
What do they think of the other person?
What did they think of themselves when it happened?
Is there a secondary gain?
What memories about the past did it evoke? What thoughts about the future came up?
What is your client's earliest memory of that statement? What do they think needs to happen for them to let go of the belief without making a conscious effort to let go of it?

### *Feelings*

What emotions came up as they considered or relived the situation?
What bodily sensations do they notice, and where? Describe the sensations in as much detail as possible.

Many people confuse emotions and thoughts with behaviors. For example, they might respond to this question by saying, "I feel nobody cares," which is not an emotion. It is helpful to use a list of emotions available for download from thework.com.

### ANGRY

enraged
malicious
infuriated
violent
vindictive
furious
repulsed
seething
scornful
hitting
yelling
revengeful
hostile
insulting
swearing
condemning
offensive
aggressive
bitter
loud
sarcastic
frustrated
resentful
critical
mean
sadistic
spiteful
jealous
short-tempered
mad
cross
retaliating
overbearing
incensed
upset
irritated
controlling
agitated
antagonistic
reprimanding
envious
reactive
abrupt
quarrelsome
stubborn
rebellious
exasperated
impatient
contrary
disrespectful
unpleasant
annoyed
dictatorial
sharp
snapping

### DEPRESSED

suicidal
directionless
empty
desperate
despairing
in hell
alienated
miserable
masochistic
despicable
self-hating
self-critical
self-deprecating
stuck
ashamed
exhausted
lousy
tired
despondent
disheartened
down
disappointed
discouraged
powerless
hopeless
grouchy
guilty
dissatisfied
sulky
low
bad
bummed out
pessimistic
dejected
glum
cheerless
rotten
crabby
resistant
punishing
morose
cranky
grumpy
burdened
negative
closed
contracted
tight
blocked
moody
out of sorts
no energy
touchy
haggard
drawn
slumped
slouching
achy
self-loathing
crummy
wretched

### CONFUSED

lost
disoriented
off-kilter
frenzied
indecisive
doubtful
uncertain
distrustful
misgiving
unsure
uneasy
tense
stressed
argumentative
authoritative
condescending
embarrassed
hesitant
shy
disillusioned
uncomfortable
comparing
dishonest
demanding
distracted
blushing
awkward
conflicted

| CONFUSED | HELPLESS | INDIFFERENT | AFRAID |
| --- | --- | --- | --- |
| lost | paralyzed | cold | terrified |
| disoriented | distraught | lifeless | petrified |
| off-kilter | doomed | uncaring | panicked |
| frenzied | distressed | uninterested | frozen |
| indecisive | pathetic | unresponsive | threatened |
| doubtful | overwhelmed | insensitive | hateful |
| uncertain | shut down | numb | agoraphobic |
| distrustful | incompetent | dull | fearful |
| misgiving | incapable | reserved | suspicious |
| unsure | alone | weary | rigid |
| uneasy | fatigued | bored | phobic |
| tense | useless | preoccupied | disturbed |
| stressed | inferior | robotic | disrupted |
| argumentative | vulnerable | slow | anxious |
| authoritative | inept | sluggish | alarmed |
| condescending | incapacitated | blasé | dreading |
| embarrassed | cut off | blank | attacking |
| hesitant | trapped | | intimidated |
| shy | weak | | nervous |
| disillusioned | sick | | scared |
| uncomfortable | nauseated | | worried |
| comparing | fidgety | | frightened |
| dishonest | trembling | | timid |
| demanding | craving | | shaky |
| distracted | squirming | | restless |
| blushing | jittery | | cowardly |
| awkward | woozy | | |
| conflicted | compulsive | | |

**AFRAID**

insecure
wary
menaced
uptight
apprehensive
defensive
guarded
troubled
self-absorbed
intolerant
avoiding
unwelcoming
unbending
paranoid
inhibited
immobile
attached
prejudiced
self-conscious

**HURT**

tormented
pained
tortured
agonized
crushed
deprived
rejected
humiliated
insulted
injured
offended
afflicted
aching
victimized
heartbroken
appalled
wronged
withdrawn
miffed
indignant
suffering
distant
invaded
bulldozed
bullied
secretive
slighted
smothered
belittled

**SAD**

anguished
desolate
devastated
grieved
tearful
sorrowful
unhappy
lonely
mournful
dismayed
downhearted
oversensitive
remorseful
sullen
sour
self-castigating
unworthy
fragile
disconnected
blindsided
discontented
crying
groaning
moaning
forlorn

**JUDGMENTAL**

stony
hurtful
brutal
combative
attacked
tactless
glaring
disgusted
ranting
scolding
obsessive
serious
stern
frowning
recoiling
unfair
bossy
stilted
stiff
pushy
neglectful
stonewalling
rude
shrill
hard
fake
phony
shallow
territorial
complaining
blunt
arrogant
superior
faultfinding

I find it helpful to have my clients go through the top headings and then work their way down the list of feelings they identify with. Or we can ask clients if they can identify any of the four primary emotions (sad, glad, mad (angry), and scared).

### *Behavior*

How do your client's thinking and emotion drive their behavior? Your client is encouraged to pay close attention to how they react outwardly (body language) and how they "want to respond" internally. I would ask them if there was a video camera in the room, what would it record (audio and video)? How do they treat the person(s) they have a conflict with?

The idea is to get your client to slow down and reflect on how the stressful belief affects them and their relationship in multiple ways.

One of the key teachings of the Buddhist philosophy is how we crave pleasant bodily sensations and try to push away unpleasant sensations. Or we get bored when the sensations are neutral. So many behaviors stem from an effort to run away from or avoid negative sensations. This is the root cause of all addictions. So, ask your client how the negative belief drives them to any addictive behaviors.

### *Outcome or Result*

What is the outcome or result of their behavior? Use the example of nobody loves me or cares about me here.

Notice how the reactions tend to reinforce the original belief. This is how your client gets stuck in a negative pattern. What can they not see or do when they attach to the belief? What happens to the relationship? In a work situation, they might get fired.

### Fourth Question:
### *Who would you be without that thought?*

The fourth question in The Work is a unique and transformative element that differentiates it from traditional cognitive therapy methods. Not only does this question serve as a hurdle for newcomers, but it also remains a point of deep introspection for those who have been practicing The Work for years. When you first pose this question to your client, don't be surprised if you're met with a look of perplexity or a response like, "What do you mean? I would still be me." This is perfectly normal and even expected.

What sets the fourth question apart is its ability to guide your client past the surface level of their thoughts and into a more experiential and visceral realm. It's not just a mental exercise; it's an invitation to reconnect with their true essence, the part of them that exists independently of their thoughts and beliefs.

Now, how can you, as a therapist, facilitate a more profound journey into this question for your client? Byron Katie often uses a straightforward but powerful technique: she invites the individual to close their eyes and vividly imagine the scenario or the person they have issues with—absent the belief that's causing distress. As a facilitator, you can encourage your client to share in great detail what they visualize, sense emotionally, and even experience somatically under these new, belief-free conditions. What changes do they notice in their interactions with the person? How does the absence of the belief impact their emotional landscape and their bodily sensations?

Providing ample time for your client to mull over this question is crucial. Rushing through this step would defeat its purpose. Allowing space for the client to delve deep will pave the way for the emergence of profound, often life-changing insights.

The fourth question sets The Work apart from Cognitive Behavioral Therapy in a fundamental way. It's not just another question; it's a potent tool, a north star guiding us back to our true nature, to the state of being that exists beyond our thoughts and concepts. Weaving this question into the fabric of your therapeutic practice can unlock a powerful pathway to deep, enduring transformation for your clients.

Like the list of words that can help someone with difficulty with feelings, Thework.com website also has a list of words to assist someone struggling with this question.

| OPEN | LOVING | HAPPY | INTERESTED |
|---|---|---|---|
| free | devoted | blissful | fascinated |
| interested | passionate | joyous | intrigued |
| receptive | considerate | delighted | absorbed |
| accepting | affectionate | overjoyed | amazed |
| kind | sensitive | gleeful | engrossed |
| harmonious | tender | elated | inquisitive |
| empathetic | attracted | jubilant | curious |
| tolerant | admiring | euphoric | involved |
| understanding | warm | thankful | attentive |
| easy | touched | festive | observant |
| connected | close | ecstatic | amused |
| sympathetic | loved | satisfied | thoughtful |
| friendly | sweet | glad | courteous |
| approachable | gentle | cheerful | intent |
| outgoing | compassionate | sunny | focused |
| flowing | caring | jovial | |
| flexible | allowing | fun-loving | |
| present | nonjudgmental | lighthearted | |
| listening | appreciative | easygoing | |
| welcoming | respectful | mellow | |
| embracing | humble | happy-go-lucky | |
| | gracious | glorious | |
| | patient | innocent | |
| | honoring | child-like | |
| | expansive | gratified | |
| | kindly | rapturous | |
| | grateful | in good humor | |
| | | in heaven | |
| | | on top of the world | |

| ALIVE | POSITIVE | PEACEFUL | STRONG |
|---|---|---|---|
| playful | inspired | calm | hardy |
| courageous | enthusiastic | content | secure |
| energetic | bold | quiet | stable |
| liberated | brave | certain | honest |
| exhilarated | daring | relaxed | reliable |
| optimistic | hopeful | serene | sure |
| frisky | exuberant | good | certain |
| animated | in the zone | at ease | dynamic |
| spirited | eager | comfortable | tenacious |
| thrilled | keen | pleased | composed |
| wonderful | earnest | encouraged | self-affirming |
| funny | upbeat | surprised | truthful |
| great | creative | bright | supportive |
| giving | constructive | blessed | excellent |
| sharing | helpful | assured | perseverant |
| intelligent | resourceful | clear | responsible |
| equal | motivated | balanced | energized |
| excited | cooperative | fine | sane |
| enjoying | productive | okay | complete |
| communicative | responsive | carefree | mature |
| active | conscientious | adequate | solid |
| spunky | approving | fulfilled | confident |
| youthful | honored | genuine | |
| vigorous | privileged | authentic | |
| tickled | adaptable | beautiful | |
| engaged | | forgiving | |
| | | sincere | |
| | | uplifted | |
| | | unburdened | |
| | | self-sufficient | |

In their book *Mindfulness-Based Cognitive Therapy for Depression,* Zindel Segal and his colleagues emphasized the importance of personal experience in mindfulness practice (Segal, 2018). They learned the hard way that teaching a practice you haven't personally engaged with can lead to ineffective and perhaps even detrimental, outcomes. The same principle applies to The Work of Byron Katie. While it may not be a strict prerequisite, having personal experience practicing The Work can profoundly enrich your ability to guide others through it.

So why is personal experience so invaluable? First, doing The Work yourself provides an intimate understanding of the method's nuances and challenges. You can more effectively navigate your clients through the four questions and the turnarounds because you've walked that path yourself. You understand the stumbling blocks, the 'aha' moments, and the deep internal shifts that can occur. This firsthand knowledge equips you with practical skills and fosters a genuine empathy for what your client is going through.

Second, practicing The Work enriches your own self-awareness and emotional intelligence. A heightened understanding of your own belief systems, thoughts, and emotions will invariably make you a more effective therapist. You can't guide someone through terrain you haven't traversed yourself or shine a light into corners of the human psyche that you haven't explored.

Lastly, doing The Work personally can act as a credibility booster. Your clients are more likely to trust the process when they know you have undertaken the same journey yourself, leading them to engage more fully and authentically.

So, while it's possible to facilitate The Work without firsthand experience, the depth of understanding and credibility that come from personal practice are invaluable assets. As you explore this transformative technique on your own, you'll be better equipped to help your clients navigate their inner worlds and come to powerful realizations that can change their lives.

## SUMMARY

- Explain the four questions process gently to clients to avoid feeling tricked or interrogated. Give them an overview first.
- The first question is, "Is it true?" Have them slow down and watch for simple yes or no answers.
- Only ask the second question "Can you absolutely know that it's true?" if they answered yes to the first. Don't let them collect evidence here.
- For the third question, "How do you react, what happens, when you believe that thought?" use the order of creation diagram—Thoughts, Feelings, Behaviors, Outcomes. Have them reflect on the sub-questions in detail.
- The fourth question, "Who would you be without that thought?" is unique and invites reconnecting with essence. Have them visualize and experience the scenario without the belief.
- Personal experience with The Work enriches therapists' skills in guiding clients through it via understanding, empathy, and credibility.
- Tools like emotions word lists can help clients articulate feelings and answer the fourth question.

# REFLECTION QUESTIONS

1. How might you explain the four questions and the overall process of The Work to a new client in a clear and gentle way? What kind of introduction would help set them at ease?

2. Can you think of a time when you pushed a client too fast through questioning? How might you adjust your approach to be more gradual and allow for pauses?

3. What feelings and reactions arise as you imagine guiding clients through the four questions? Do you notice any resistance or fear? How might you work with those feelings?

4. How have you experienced the power of the fourth question in your own life? What insights arose when you asked, "Who would you be without that belief?"

5. Do you feel practicing The Work yourself before using it with clients would be beneficial? What might you gain from doing so?

# CHAPTER 6

## The Work as a Meditation

The Work is meditation in action, a dynamic process of inquiry. Let me highlight a few essential steps to help your clients succeed with this approach. Just as in meditation, invite your clients to close their eyes if they feel comfortable and encourage them to find inner stillness. Guide them to observe what arises within as they sit with each question. Some clients, especially those with an overactive mind, may ask you to repeat the question. That's okay. Remind your clients to release any preconceived notions about "right" or expected answers. If they approach the questions sincerely and patiently, allowing themselves to explore genuinely, the answers will emerge naturally, often catching them by surprise.

There is a "place" beyond thoughts that exists within all of us. This is the place of silence and wisdom accessible to all if we allow ourselves to be quiet and go beyond the invisible yet persistent wall of our thoughts and assumptions. With practice and genuine sincerity, you can guide your clients to this silent presence with no name because it is before thoughts and memories. It is a living space.

My meditation teacher Mr. Goenka's deep baritone voice, rings in my ears as I write these words. He extorts the meditation students to have the three P's—patience, persistence, and practice as they learn to meditate. He compares the Vipassana meditation he teaches to surgery. Just as a surgeon carefully removes diseased tissue and pus to promote healing, Vipassana meditation helps practitioners release the ingrained somatic patterns of craving and aversion that cause suffering. This process can be intense and uncomfortable at times, much like surgery, but it is necessary for the attainment of lasting peace and happiness. The Work is also a deep surgery that will help your client let go of their deeply held beliefs that are causing them suffering and holding them back in their lives and important relationships. Katie sometimes compares it to learning to ride a bike. The Work will come to you with patience, persistence, and practice.

One of the key revelations to me when I experienced The Work for the first time with my friend Celeste was a powerful somatic shift. I felt a wonderful physical release as I went deeper into inquiry with her gentle guidance. Let The Work reveal to you and your clients the road less traveled into the pathless land of the unknown and unknowable. Both you and your client will be glad for it.

### Time and Mental Health

Most of us struggle with accepting reality as it is. We often find ourselves trapped in a web of painful memories, tangled in guilt and regret. Our minds may race with anxiety or fear when we contemplate the future. We cling to the hope that happiness lies just around the corner, waiting for us in some anticipated event or achievement. But here's the thing: when we're lost in ruminations about the past or consumed by worries about the future, we're missing out on the only moment we truly have—the present. The real magic, the opportunity for joy and peace, lies in embracing the here and now.

Out of the three subdivisions illustrated above, neither the past nor the future exists as realities. They come into existence only when there is a movement of thoughts as memories or imagination. Learning from our past experiences is essential, and it would be helpful to plan for the future. However, dwelling in the past or the future is not advisable or practical.

Recent studies have shown that rumination is the leading cause of depression. Similarly, anxiety is a byproduct of constantly worrying about the future. (Michl et al., 2013). We do not have any control over the past or the future. In other words, we cannot choose what we feel or think.

The present moment is the most vital aspect of time because this is where all our actions occur. Everything we value—connection, peace, love, beauty, etc., is not a product of thought and therefore is always in the present.

So, what is the secret that would help someone to be in the present moment? Our painful memories of the past and fearful thoughts about the future get traction only if we engage them or believe them. The Work is a powerful tool for identifying and questioning those beliefs that tend to move us out of this moment.

## The Importance of Writing

For almost a year after I discovered The Work, I used to do the inquiry in my mind most of the time. I see many of my clients also doing the same. There are many reasons why it is more beneficial to do The Work in writing or have a facilitator guide:

- Thoughts are elusive, and as we investigate them, they can get very distracting, making it hard to stay focused. If we do The Work in writing, returning to where we got distracted is easier.
- It is impossible to write as fast as we think. Therefore, the process of writing tends to slow us down and slow down our thoughts.
- Writing gives form to thoughts so we can focus on and work on them.

- I have often noticed that writing fearful thoughts on paper does not feel as scary as it did when I was thinking about them.
- Lastly, the thoughts in our heads tend to be repetitive. The tendency to repeat them is drastically minimized when we write them down.

### Understanding the Three Kinds of Business

The concept of the "three kinds of business"—mine, yours, and God's or nature's—offered by Byron Katie is a transformative tool you can easily integrate into your psychotherapeutic practice. It provides an elegant yet powerful framework for clients to reframe stress, anxiety, and emotional suffering. The underlying premise is straightforward yet profound: much of our emotional turmoil stems from mentally meddling in businesses that aren't ours.

Here are some examples. When I am telling my friend he should break up with their partner or when I am gossiping about a neighbor's personal life, I am in their business. I am in God's business when I am worrying about natural disasters.

Let's delve deeper into this. Imagine your client is ruminating over a recent interaction where they felt unheard or dismissed. They might be agonizing over what the other person thinks of them. The question "Whose business am I in when I believe that thought?" can be a game-changer. It can swiftly refocus your client's energy and attention back to what is within their realm of control—their own business.

When clients invest their mental and emotional energy into other people's actions, thoughts, or feelings—or even the uncontrollable circumstances dictated by nature—they inadvertently relinquish control over their emotional state. And what's the result? Stress, anxiety, and even a sense of loneliness because no one is left to attend to their own business—their own needs, feelings, and well-being.

This is not to advocate for emotional isolationism but to emphasize emotional responsibility. Yes, your interactions with others are important, and yes, you exist in a broader context of societal and natural phenomena. However, the primary business that you have any real authority or control over is your own. Redirecting focus this way can alleviate much of the emotional weight clients may carry.

This principle is especially beneficial for clients dealing with codependency issues, boundary problems, or those who simply find themselves frequently stressed by external circumstances and other people's behaviors. It's also an empowering framework for anyone navigating the complexities of personal, familial, or professional relationships.

Integrating the "three kinds of business" into your therapeutic practice can offer clients a simple, relatable way to compartmentalize their concerns and focus on what they can influence. It fosters emotional autonomy and resilience, equipping your clients with the perspective they need to navigate life's complexities more efficiently. By adopting this straightforward yet profound approach, both you and your clients can work towards emotional clarity and a more grounded sense of self.

## SUMMARY

- The inquiry process in The Work is similar to meditation.
- Encourage clients to be patient, persistent, and practice.
- The Work can lead to somatic shifts and personal growth.
- Time and mental health: Practicing The Work can help us avoid dwelling in the past or future and focus on the present moment.
- The Work helps identify and question beliefs that move us out of the present moment.
- Writing is essential for staying focused and giving form to thoughts.
- Understand the three kinds of business: mine, yours, and God's/nature's.
- Focusing on one's own business reduces stress and suffering.

# REFLECTION QUESTIONS

1. What came up for you as you read about being present and letting go of the past and future? Were you able to relate to the struggle of dwelling on what was or what could be? How might this chapter help you be more present with your clients?

2. Did you connect with writing thoughts down rather than just thinking them? What benefits of writing stood out to you? How might you incorporate more writing into your practice or suggest it to clients?

3. What was your reaction to the concept of the "three kinds of business"—yours, others, and God's/nature's? Could you relate to the stress of mentally entering into others' business? How might you apply this framework of recognizing whose business you are in with clients?

4. As you reflect on the fundamental principles in this chapter—being present, inquiry through writing, and understanding different kinds of business—which resonated with you the most? Why? How might you apply or experiment with this in your life and practice?

5. After reading this chapter, what is one key insight or take-away you have? How might this shape your therapeutic approach going forward?

# PART III

# USING TW WITH SPECIFIC DIAGNOSIS AND CLINICAL SITUATIONS

In the following chapters, we will explore how to use The Work in psychotherapy to address specific diagnostic categories and clinical presentations. Because of space limitations, not all diagnoses outlined in the Diagnostic and Statistical Manual of Mental Disorders (DSM) will be covered. Instead, we will focus on those commonly encountered in clinical settings, excluding categories such as neurodevelopmental disorders, motor disorders, psychotic disorders, dissociative disorders, sleep disorders, and a few others.

The clinical dialogues between the therapist and clients have been modified for brevity and clarity while preserving the client's confidentiality.

# CHAPTER 7

## Addictions

It is important to recognize that addictions can have both biological and psychological components. While some people may be more genetically predisposed to addiction, and some substances contain ingredients that are physiologically addictive, such as nicotine, opiates, and alcohol, environmental and psychological factors can also play a role in the development of addictive behaviors. Substances like alcohol, nicotine, and opioids release dopamine, creating reward circuits in the brain that reinforce addictive behaviors. Withdrawal symptoms that arise when stopping substance use are tied to neurochemical changes as the brain adjusts to functioning without the substance.

While cognitive techniques don't eliminate biological components of addiction, they can help clients manage cravings and avoid triggers. Integrating both psychological and pharmacological approaches is often most effective for treating addictions holistically. The Work provides a psychological tool to complement medical and biological treatment methods aimed at restoring healthy brain functioning. Additionally, it is important to recognize that people can become addicted not only to substances such as drugs and alcohol but also to behaviors such as exercise, pornography, shopping, or work. In my own experience, I've found The Work especially effective in treating these behavioral addictions.

I recall a discussion with Dr. Alan Marlatt, a former colleague and friend specializing in addictive behaviors research. Alan had recently completed a 10-day Meditation Retreat with the renowned Vipassana teacher, Mr. Goenka. During their conversation, Mr. Goenka conveyed to Alan that all addictions are essentially a form of addiction to thinking.

In the realm of our clinical work, understanding addiction is vital. Let's be candid: at the heart of addiction lies a universal quest for self-improvement and fulfillment. Yes, we're all addicts in some form, hooked on the narrative we've spun about who we are and who we ought to be. We're addicted not just to substances or behaviors but fundamentally to our self-concepts.

So, what's the issue? The drive that fuels our addictions can never deliver lasting satisfaction. The gratification is fleeting whether you achieve professional success, establish fulfilling relationships, or even reach spiritual enlightenment. Then what? The search resumes, and the cycle continues. We're perpetually chasing the next 'high,' be it material or spiritual.

Why does this happen? Because our addictions are essentially misguided attempts to fill a perceived void within us. We're searching for completeness in external things—drugs, experiences, relationships—when true completeness can't be outsourced. It's like grasping at air; what you seek always seems to elude you.

This can lead to a crisis point, where the disillusionment with external achievements begins to sink in. But this isn't necessarily a dead end. It's often the first step toward a profound realization: the wholeness we seek is already within us in each moment. We've been looking in the wrong direction, identifying with the wave when we are, in fact, the entire ocean.

Think of addictions as a twisted form of yearning for the one thing that truly matters: unconditional love. But here's the kicker: we are that unconditional love. No substance or external validation can provide the totality of acceptance and love that already resides within us. Even in your darkest moments as a therapist or in the most challenging sessions with your clients, that essence remains pure and unscathed.

So, what's the takeaway for your practice? Incorporating an understanding of addiction as a quest for wholeness and unconditional love can fundamentally shift how you approach treatment. Techniques like The Work of Byron Katie can be instrumental in helping clients dismantle the self-concepts that fuel their addictions, guiding them back to their inherent completeness. This isn't just about breaking a cycle; it's about awakening to a more accurate, holistic understanding of self. Wouldn't you want to facilitate that kind of transformative journey for your clients?

I have observed an increase in the prevalence of work addiction in recent years, particularly with the blurring of boundaries between the office and home as a result of the pandemic and the shift towards remote work.

The rise of workaholism in modern society is taking its toll on workers and their families. People driven to work excessively often find themselves so consumed by their goals that they don't take time for rest or self-care. As if this weren't bad enough, many of these individuals also turn to substance abuse to cope with their relentless pressure.

Studies have found that people who become addicted to work may be more likely than others to use alcohol or drugs to escape from the pressures they face. This dependence on substances can lead them into a vicious cycle where they rely more heavily on drugs or alcohol to keep up with their daily tasks at work. Some researchers argue that those who are addicted may be self-medicating their anxiety or depression to stay focused on their jobs. This kind of behavior increases the risk of developing an addiction even further since substance use can become a coping mechanism for dealing with stressors related to work performance. Long-term substance abuse has been linked with cognitive decline, which could further impair an individual's ability to function socially and professionally at optimal levels.

Let us look at the example of Michele, a successful manager addicted to her work. Michele believes that she needs to work all the time to be successful. This belief has led her to work long hours, even when exhausted. She doesn't take breaks, and she neglects her health. Her obsession with work is causing her a great deal of suffering, but she couldn't see it because she believes she is wasting her time. Michele grew up in a strict Catholic household where her mom repeatedly said, "Idle hands are the devil's workshop." This belief was so ingrained in her that she found it impossible to relax. Even when she was on vacation, she would work long hours. Michele's addiction to work led to many problems in her life. Her belief that she needs to work all the time to be successful has neglected her health and well-being, led to professional burnout. Despite her hard work, she still felt stuck in a rut and wasn't getting any closer to achieving her goals. Eventually, the strain of it all became too much for her, and she found herself exhausted, overwhelmed, and feeling like she needed help, which is when she came to me.

Having grown up in a strict Catholic household where seeking therapy was seen as a sign of weakness, Michele struggled to reconcile her beliefs with the idea of seeking help. Additionally, her deeply held belief that she needed to work all the time to be successful made it difficult for her to see the value in taking time for herself and addressing her mental health. Despite these reservations, Michele eventually decided to try The Work, recognizing that her obsession with work was causing her significant suffering and that she needed to find a way to manage her stress and improve her well-being.

Michele's beliefs are relatively common among many I have worked with. I am listing below some of the more common beliefs I have encountered. Unfortunately, these beliefs have recently become more pronounced as many tech workers are getting laid off. Society tends to reward many of these beliefs, and to a certain extent, the belief that one must be constantly working could help an individual succeed in her career. Taken to an extreme, like in the case of Michele, these beliefs can have the opposite effect—leading to unnecessary burnout, procrastination, and relationship problems. Here is a list of some of the more frequent beliefs I've encountered:

### Underlying Beliefs of Workaholics:

1. Working long hours is the only way to be successful and achieve one's goals.
2. Taking a break from work shows weakness and failure.
3. Becoming too tired to keep working means not meeting your expectations or keeping up with the competition.
4. Financial security is more important than anything else, including mental health, physical health, and time with family and friends.
5. Hard work will always pay off, even if it takes a lot of effort and sacrifice in the short term.
6. Your worth as an individual is measured by your productivity or success at work.

7. You must endure suffering to succeed, including exhaustion and neglecting other areas of life, such as health or relationships.
8. Having fewer hobbies beyond work is better because it allows one to focus on succeeding at one's job or career more easily and quickly.
9. Perfectionism may lead to rewards such as job promotions or additional compensation for outstanding work performance rather than enhancing the quality of personal relationships outside of work, such as those with family or friends.
10. It's essential to appear busy even when there's nothing productive happening to maintain your competitive edge over others who may also be vying for similar opportunities at work.

It is important to note that the beliefs listed above, taken to an extreme, can have detrimental effects on an individual's personal and familial relationships. This is particularly true for women, who often shoulder the responsibilities of maintaining a career and caring for the home and children. This phenomenon, known as the "double shift," can lead to feelings of guilt and inadequacy for women who strive to excel in both their professional and personal roles. Additionally, societal norms and expectations often hold women to a higher standard of caregiving, leading to negative perceptions and judgments when they prioritize their careers over their families. These societal beliefs and pressures can further exacerbate the harmful effects of workaholism on women's mental and emotional well-being.

Here is an example of how some clients' tenacious beliefs can affect their thinking and behavior. The following conversation demonstrates how a therapist can introduce The Work to a workaholic client who may resist examining their beliefs about work and productivity.

Michele: "I don't know if I'm ready for this. I've always believed that I need to work all the time to succeed. It's just how I was raised."

Therapist: "I understand that it can be difficult to let go of deeply held beliefs, but it's important to question them if they no longer work for you. Can we question your assumption, "I need to work all the time to be successful?"

Michele: "I guess I just don't want to waste my time. And I'm afraid that I'll fall behind or lose my edge if I'm not working all the time."

Therapist: "I can see how you are attached to that belief. Would you be willing to put that belief to inquiry through The Work? Is it true that you must work all the time to succeed?"

Michele: "Not really, no. I guess I'm just afraid that if I stop working, I'll lose everything I've worked for."

Therapist: "How do you react to this belief? What happens when you believe you need to work all the time to be successful?"

Michele: "Okay, I'll try. (pauses) When I believe the thought,' I need to work all the time to be successful,' I feel anxious and stressed. I neglect my health and well-being and struggle to relax or enjoy my time off."

Therapist: "It sounds like you feel a lot of pressure when you believe you need to work all the time to be successful. How does this pressure manifest in your daily life?"

Michele: "Well, I constantly check and respond to emails, even when I'm not at work. I have difficulty disconnecting and feel guilty if I take a break. I also find myself sacrificing my needs, like exercising or seeing friends and family, to put more time into work. It's like I'm constantly running on a hamster wheel, and I can't get off."

Therapist: "It sounds like this belief negatively affects your overall well-being and quality of life. Do you think this belief is helping you or hindering you from achieving your goals?"

Michele: "I think it's hindering me. Even though I'm putting in all this extra time and effort, I'm not necessarily seeing the results I want. And I'm so exhausted and burnt out all the time that I don't have the energy to give my best effort at work."

Therapist: "It seems like this belief may not be serving you well. Who would you be without the belief I need to work all the time to be successful?"

Michele: "Without that belief, I think I would feel less stressed and overwhelmed. I would probably have more energy to put toward work and other areas of my life. I might be able to enjoy my time off more and have better relationships with the people around me. I might also be able to set more realistic goals for myself and feel more fulfilled and satisfied with my achievements."

Therapist: "Great. Are you ready to turn the thought around? What is the simple opposite of that thought? Also, give me some examples of the opposite."

Michele: "I don't need to work all the time to be successful. I can use my time off to rest and recharge, which can lead to increased productivity and creativity when I return to work. I can use my time off to pursue personal interests or hobbies, bringing me joy and fulfillment and potentially leading to new opportunities or career paths."

Therapist: "Excellent examples. It's important to find a balance between work and other aspects of your life and take care of your physical and mental health to achieve long-term success."

Michele: "Smiling broadly—I can see that clearly now."

After some strong initial resistance, we narrowed down some of Michele's closely held beliefs about her work life. We started by questioning her core belief: "Taking a break from work is a sign of weakness and failure." She was so convinced about this belief that she answered the first two questions of The Work—Is it true? And can you absolutely know that it is true?—with a resounding "Yes." However, by honestly answering question #3 (How do you react, what happens, when you believe that thought?), she could see how holding onto the belief was causing her a lot of physical and emotional stress. She could reckon the price she paid for neglecting her personal care and not spending time with the people she cared about. Michele also had difficulty with the turnaround to the opposite of her belief—"taking a break from work is a sign of strength."

The Work was a game-changer for Michele. It gave her the tools to finally confront the beliefs fueling her unhealthy obsession with work and success. Through this process, she began to recognize and challenge the negative thought patterns running the show, driving her to constantly push herself to the brink of burnout. As she dug deeper, Michele started to uncover a new perspective that allowed her to pursue her goals in a more balanced, fulfilling way. She realized that she could still work hard and strive for success, but she didn't have to sacrifice her entire life in the process. Slowly but surely, Michele started making time for what mattered: taking breaks to recharge, rediscovering hobbies that brought her joy, and nurturing her relationships with family and friends. The Work helped Michele find a sense of equilibrium, showing her that true success isn't just about grinding away at work—it's about creating a life that feels rich, meaningful, and authentically her own.

As psychotherapists, we are no strangers to the intricacies of addictions that are rooted in both psychological and biological factors. Whether it's alcohol, drugs, or any other substance, the equation is never simple. A complex interplay of emotional cravings, chemical imbalances, and social factors makes this a difficult cycle to break. You've likely seen clients make progress only to relapse, sometimes despite their best intentions. And let's face it, traditional therapeutic interventions can often be limited in their efficacy for such deeply rooted issues.

I would like to share with you an example of doing The Work with Alex, who was struggling with his alcohol use.

This is an abbreviated version of a session with Alex, who has been struggling with his alcohol use for six years. Alex enters the room, looking nervous. He takes a deep breath, trying to calm his shaky nerves.

Therapist: "Welcome, Alex. It's good to see you today. Please, take a seat."

Alex: "Thanks for having me. I've heard a lot about The Work, but I'm still uncertain how it can help me."

Therapist: "It's a process of inquiry, Alex. It helps you question the thoughts that cause you suffering. Through it, you might find peace with yourself and your relationship with alcohol. Let's begin, shall we?"

Alex: Nods "All right."

Therapist: "First, think of a thought or belief about your relationship with alcohol that causes you stress or pain."

Alex: Takes a moment, then mumbles: "I need alcohol to cope with my life."

Therapist: "Thank you for sharing that, Alex. Let's investigate this thought together. First question: Is it true that you need alcohol to cope with your life?"

Alex: Pauses. "It feels true... but I guess deep down, I know it's not."

Therapist: "And how do you react, what happens, when you believe that thought?"

Alex: "I feel trapped. I rely on alcohol even more. I feel ashamed, weak, and distant from my loved ones."

Therapist: "And who would you be without that thought? Imagine your life without the belief that you need alcohol to cope."

Alex: A tear rolls down his cheek. "I'd be free. I'd be present for my family. I'd feel stronger and more capable of handling life's challenges."

Therapist: "Now, let's turn the thought to its opposite."

Alex: "Can you help me with that?"

Therapist: "Sure. Instead of 'I need alcohol to cope with my life,' what if the thought was 'I don't need alcohol to cope with my life'? Can you find three genuine examples of when this might be true?"

Alex: "1. When I play with my daughter, I forget about my cravings. 2. When I'm engrossed in my hobbies, like painting, I feel content without alcohol. 3. There have been days when I've managed stress at work without turning to a drink."

Therapist: "Beautiful, Alex. This inquiry is just the beginning. Every time you notice the stressful thought arising, ask yourself these questions. Let yourself feel and explore. Remember, this isn't about denying or fighting the thought but understanding it."

Alex: "It's so enlightening. I've always felt chained by that belief. Thank you."

Therapist: "You're welcome, Alex. Keep questioning. Keep diving deep. You have the strength within to find your truth."

So, are you ready to expand your toolkit and possibly change how you approach addictions in your practice? You may find that this approach offers a complementary lens through which your clients can explore, question, and potentially transform the beliefs that fuel their addictive behaviors.

# REFLECTION QUESTIONS

1. When have you seen clients struggle with work addiction or self-medication due to rigidly held beliefs? How could The Work help them challenge those beliefs?

2. How might you introduce The Work to clients who resist therapy or hold strong beliefs that therapy is a sign of weakness? What advice does this chapter offer?

3. In what ways have you seen societal expectations and gender roles impact women's susceptibility to work addiction or lack of work-life balance? How can The Work help address these systemic issues?

4. What might be some obstacles or challenges to implementing The Work with clients struggling with work addiction? How does the case study of Michele provide solutions or advice for overcoming those obstacles?

5. How can concepts from Buddhist psychology, like impermanence and non-attachment, complement The Work in addressing issues like addiction, anxiety, and workaholism? What connections do you see between the two approaches?

6. What resonated with you most in the case study and description of how The Work helped Michele? How might you apply those insights to your clients?

# CHAPTER 8

## Anxiety

In today's fast-paced world, anxiety disorders are skyrocketing, and let's face it—conventional therapies and medications don't always cut it. As a seasoned psychotherapist, I know the importance of having diverse, practical approaches at your disposal.

Consider Brett's case below as a prime example. Utilizing The Work, Brett was guided to interrogate and dismantle his negative beliefs. The result? A transformative shift in perspective that alleviated his crippling anxiety. This isn't an isolated case; it illustrates how The Work can be a game-changer in your practice.

Are you worried about the alarming rates of anxiety among college students? You're not alone. The stresses of contemporary college life are pushing more students towards emotional turmoil. But remember, anxiety is a universal issue, transcending age, background, and education. Recognizing that anxiety wears many faces is vital. Tailoring your treatment plans to individual client needs isn't just good practice; it's essential.

Brett had always been a bit anxious. But it wasn't until he started college that his anxiety began to take over his life. He would constantly worry about everything, from his grades to his close relationships and his future. He would avoid social situations at all costs and spend most of his time alone in his room. The thought of speaking in front of a group or even just answering a question in class made him feel sick to his stomach.

His anxiety was so debilitating that it began to affect his schoolwork. He started getting lower grades and began to doubt himself more and more. He was convinced that he would never be good enough and would never achieve his goals.

One day, Brett hit rock bottom. He was sitting in his room, surrounded by all his unfinished work, when he had a panic attack. He felt like he couldn't breathe, and he felt his heart racing. He was soon convinced that he was going to die. The experience was so terrifying that he decided to make an appointment for therapy.

During his intake appointment, he kept repeating that he would never be good enough. He would say things like, "I'm not smart enough," "I'm not talented enough," or "I'll never be successful." I asked him why he believed these things, and he said it was because of his upbringing in a family of high achievers. He told me that his anxiety made him doubt himself constantly and that he felt like he was always on the verge of a panic attack.

We started questioning his assumption, "I am not good enough." Brett could see how he experienced a range of negative emotions and behaviors when he believed that thought. He described feelings of insecurity, low self-esteem, self-doubt, inadequacy, and feelings of failure. He reported engaging in self-defeating behaviors, such as procrastinating and avoiding challenges, or new experiences. He would easily give up on his goals and dreams because he was attached to the belief that he was not good enough. He could see clearly how that belief was limiting his potential and happiness.

Without the belief, Brett could see how he would be more confident, positive, and hopeful about his future. He spoke of how, without the belief that he wasn't good enough, he would be more resilient in the face of challenges and setbacks.

When he turned the belief to "I am good enough," he initially had trouble coming up with examples for the turnaround. But very quickly, he could see himself engaging in more positive behaviors, such as setting goals for himself, working toward his self-improvement, and overall feeling more empowered and capable of achieving his goals and leading a fulfilling and meaningful life. As he came up with more real-life examples for the statement, I am good enough, his anxiety significantly decreased, and he no longer felt controlled by it. After working through the turnarounds, I sent Brett home with instructions on doing the inquiry at home. As he practiced The Work at home using real-life examples, he got better at identifying the beliefs that were causing him anxiety and began to challenge them on his own.

I'm happy to report that Brett's anxiety has significantly decreased since we started working together. He can now participate in class, answer questions, and give presentations. He still has bad days here and there, but he knows how to manage his anxiety and is no longer controlled by it.

It's great to see Brett's progress in managing his anxiety. However, it's important to recognize that anxiety is a common issue among college students. A survey conducted by the American College Health Association found that 58% of college students reported feeling overwhelming anxiety in the past year (Association, 2018). This finding highlights the need for resources and support for students struggling with anxiety, as it can have a significant impact on their academic and personal lives.

College is a time of significant transitions, from living on your own for the first time to being responsible for your education, and these changes can be difficult for some people to adjust to. Many students come to campus these days already taking anxiety medications. According to a 2018 study by the American Psychological Association, nearly 40% of college students reported experiencing symptoms of an anxiety disorder in the past year. This rate increased significantly from ten years ago when only 25% of college students reported such symptoms.

This increase in anxiety disorders among college students can likely be attributed to several different factors. One potential explanation is that college students are exposed to an increasing array of stressors, such as the pressures of excelling academically, financial insecurity, and career uncertainty. While it is true that college students have always faced a range of stressors, it is also essential to recognize that the nature and intensity of these stressors may have changed over time.

Let's unpack some of these modern challenges and outline some ways The Work could help alleviate their burden:

- **Financial Strain:** The skyrocketing costs of higher education are leading to unprecedented financial strain. When students are preoccupied with how to afford next semester's tuition, can we expect them to be mentally present in a therapy session? How can The Work help them shift their perspectives on financial insecurity?
- **Traumatic Events:** Trauma shapes us, and the core stories that emerge from traumatic experiences often serve as mental blueprints, guiding our reactions and beliefs. These stories are pivotal in the psychopathology of disorders like depression and anxiety. The Work offers a robust framework to challenge these limiting beliefs, leading to mental clarity and emotional freedom.

- **The Social Media Paradox:** For all its connective power, social media often serves as a breeding ground for self-doubt and comparison. The Work can help clients navigate the emotional pitfalls of the digital age, offering a pathway to genuine self-acceptance.
- **The COVID-19 Aftermath:** The pandemic has fundamentally altered the college experience, contributing to heightened levels of stress and anxiety. The Work can assist in reframing the narrative around these disruptions, transforming them from insurmountable challenges into opportunities for growth.
- **Political and Social Overwhelm:** Today's college students are deeply invested in societal issues—politics, social justice, and the environment. These concerns, while valid, can also be sources of intense stress. The Work provides the emotional scaffolding to manage this overwhelm, channeling it into constructive action.

So, given this plethora of modern stressors, isn't it imperative to have a tool as versatile and effective as The Work? It's not just another therapeutic technique; it's an essential skill for navigating the complexities of modern life—for both your clients and you.

The escalating rates of anxiety disorders among college students are more than just alarming statistics; they represent a tangible crisis affecting both mental and physical health. As therapists, we're often the first line of defense. Our toolkit might include traditional therapy, medication, or, sometimes, a blend of both. But what if we could offer something more transformative?

Take Brett, for example. His journey with anxiety wasn't just alleviated through medication or standard cognitive-behavioral techniques. He experienced a breakthrough with The Work, fundamentally challenging and reframing his negative beliefs. Now imagine applying that same transformative power to the myriad of students wrestling with their mental health issues. Could Brett's success story be replicated across campuses?

But let's not pigeonhole this. Anxiety isn't a "college issue" or a "youth issue"; it's a human issue. The takeaway here is customization. Anxiety doesn't have a one-size-fits-all manifestation, so why should our treatment approach? Tailoring treatment plans to individual needs isn't just best practice; it's the cornerstone of effective therapy. Integrating The Work into your therapeutic approach adds a layer of customization that can deeply empower your clients.

## REFLECTION QUESTIONS

1. How might you incorporate The Work into your practice with clients struggling with anxiety? What specific techniques or applications of The Work could be most beneficial?

2. What stood out in Brett's case study and his experience using The Work to overcome anxiety? What lessons can you take away to apply with your clients?

3. How might you adapt the techniques of The Work to be suitable for clients from diverse backgrounds, ages, and with different types of anxiety disorders? What considerations would you need to make?

# CHAPTER 9

## Abusive Relationships

Many dynamics and factors can contribute to an abusive relationship. Some of the most common include a lack of communication, feelings of insecurity or jealousy, power imbalances, and unresolved conflict.

Abusive relationships often involve a cycle of escalation and de-escalation. During the escalation phase, tension and conflict build up, and the abuse may become more frequent or severe. This is often followed by a period of de-escalation, where the violence decreases or stops altogether. However, this usually only lasts briefly before the cycle begins again.

There are many reasons why someone might stay in an abusive relationship. Some may feel they deserve the abuse or can't do any better. Others may be afraid of what will happen if they try to leave, especially given how often women are killed after leaving their abusive partners, as well as the economic impact of divorce or separation. A person may also stay in an abusive relationship because they love their partner and hope that things will change.

Below, you'll find a list of beliefs that often keep individuals anchored in abusive relationships:

- I am unlovable.
- I need him/her to make me happy.
- S/he doesn't understand me.

- S/he should listen to me.
- I have to do everything.
- I know what is best for my partner.
- Something terrible is going to happen to him/her.
- S/he shouldn't lie.
- S/he will leave me if I .......
- I am doing all the work in this relationship.
- S/he needs to make more money.
- I can't do anything right.
- I can disappoint him/her.

Almost every married and unmarried couple I've worked with has experienced conflict in their marital relationship. Marriage is a complex partnership that requires time, commitment, and communication to maintain a healthy partnership. Unfortunately, these vital components of marriage are sometimes overshadowed by chronic emotional abuse such as verbal attacks, insults, and humiliation. This type of abuse can often be the precursor to physical violence that is repeated over and over again.

Chronic emotional abuse in marriages involves power dynamics where one partner attempts to control the other through intimidation, fear tactics, and manipulation. Constant criticism and ridicule can chip away at a person's self-confidence while eroding the bonds of trust between two people who are supposed to love one another unconditionally. The abuser may use various strategies to make the victim feel powerless or insignificant, such as withholding money or attention or making decisions without consulting their partner.

The escalation from chronic emotional abuse to repeated physical violence is a situation we should never take lightly. Physical violence is unacceptable in any relationship; however, it is especially concerning when it becomes part of an ongoing pattern of domestic abuse. Victims may feel trapped as they are subjected to threats or even acts of physical aggression such as hitting, punching, slapping, kicking, or pushing. It can be challenging for victims of physical abuse to reach out for help due to feelings of shame and guilt or worries about potential retaliation from their abuser if they do speak up.

Here is an example of a couple I saw a few years ago.

Mark, a 40-year-old father of three children, was married to Beth. He was a successful sales manager for a grocery chain. He was the sole breadwinner while Beth raised their three children. After the children grew up and became independent, Beth decided to get a Master's degree in Business Administration and did her internship in the same company where Mark worked as a sales manager. Everything went well until Beth completed her training and was offered an executive position in the company. Her salary was significantly higher than Mark's income as a manager. Within a few months, Mark started getting severe backaches and had to go on disability. He became depressed and began to drink heavily. Beth was now the primary breadwinner and decision-maker in their family.

One day, after coming home from work, Beth found Mark passed out on the couch with an empty bottle of liquor by his side. She woke him up and asked him what was going on. Mark became angry and started yelling at Beth, calling her names and telling her that she was a terrible wife and mother. He accused her of not respecting him now that she was making more money than he made. After a terrible argument, they both decided to seek help.

Mark was quite adamant about his belief—Beth does not respect me. As I guided him through The Work, he was able to see how he treated her when he believed that thought, and most importantly, he saw the price he was paying for hanging onto that belief without a shred of evidence. As we looked at the examples for the turnarounds: a) *I* don't respect Beth, b) Beth *does* respect me, Mark began to sob and felt closer to Beth. However, he was shocked by his turnaround to himself—"I don't respect myself." His sobbing became uncontrollable as he gave examples from his life, starting at a young age, of how he never respected himself and always projected the lack of respect onto others. After doing The Work for a few weeks, Mark stopped abusing Beth and began to treat her as an equal partner in their relationship, and he stopped drinking. His back pain also disappeared, and they grew closer as a couple.

The Work can be effective in dealing with abuse when the abuser is willing to confront their beliefs and behaviors and is open to change. In Mark's case, he recognized his lack of respect for himself and his wife and made significant changes in his behavior. However, it's important to note that this process requires the abuser's willingness to change and their commitment to the process.

However, there are red flags that suggest the abused partner is in danger and needs to get out. These include escalation of violence, power imbalances, and a cycle of escalation and de-escalation. The abused partner may also hold onto beliefs such as feeling unlovable, believing they deserve the abuse, or fearing what will happen if they leave. Chronic emotional abuse, such as verbal attacks, insults, and humiliation, can often be a precursor to physical violence. The escalation from chronic emotional abuse to repeated physical violence is a situation that should never be taken lightly.

In such cases, the therapist must recognize these signs and guide the abused partner toward resources that can help them safely leave the abusive relationship. It's also important to remember that the economic impact of divorce or separation, as well as the fear of retaliation from the abuser, can make it difficult for the victim to leave. Therefore, providing support and resources to help the victim navigate these challenges is essential.

# REFLECTION QUESTIONS

1. How might you help clients in abusive relationships uncover and question their own underlying beliefs that keep them trapped?

2. As therapists, we also have beliefs and judgments about abuse. What beliefs might you hold about victims or abusers that could be investigated? How could questioning your own beliefs support you in being fully present for clients?

3. The example with Mark and Beth illustrates how our core beliefs about ourselves often underlie our judgments of others. How might you help clients get to the root of their self-judgments? What kind of probing questions could you ask to help clients uncover self-concepts?

4. Mark's back pain and depression lifted after questioning his beliefs through The Work. How might you explain the mind-body connection to clients whose physical symptoms could be rooted in thought? What examples resonate most with your experience?

# CHAPTER 10

## Cancer, Illness, and Disabilities

A few years ago, my colleague Grace and I ran a group in Seattle for cancer patients in various stages of their treatment. The participants were all women ranging from ages 30-70 years. Some of them had recurrences, and one had three different types of cancers in her life. One would expect this group to be very somber, but as the brave women worked through their lists of beliefs about their illness and how it affected their lives, the atmosphere in the group changed. There were a lot of tears and laughter as these courageous women worked through their beliefs and got relief from the assumptions restricting their precious lives and robbing them of joy. I will never forget the privilege of guiding them through The Work questions and the turnarounds.

Here is an example of a session with Janet:

Therapist: "Janet, how are you feeling today?"

Janet: "I'm feeling a bit overwhelmed. I'm scared that my cancer may come back, and I'm struggling to come to terms with it."

Therapist: "I understand. It can be tough to deal with a fear of the recurrence of cancer. I want to remind you that you are not alone in this and that you have the support of the group. Have you tried doing The Work with your overwhelming thoughts?"

Janet: "I've heard of it, but I'm not sure I understand what it is."

Therapist: "The Work is a simple yet powerful process of self-inquiry. Would you like to give it a try?"

Janet: "I think so. I'm willing to try anything that might help me feel better."

Therapist: "Great. Let's start by identifying a thought or belief that is causing you distress."

Janet: "It could be something like, 'I can't handle this cancer coming back.'"

Therapist: "Once you have identified the thought, we can use The Work to question it and determine if it's true for you."

Janet: "Okay. I'll try. My belief is that I can't handle this cancer coming back. It feels like it's too much to bear."

Therapist: "That's understandable. The first step is to ask yourself if it is true."

Janet: "Yes."

Therapist: "Okay. Can you absolutely know that it is true?"

Janet: "No."

Therapist: "How do you react, what happens, when you believe that you can't handle cancer coming back?"

Janet: "When I believe that I can't handle the cancer coming back, I feel overwhelmed and helpless. I start to worry about all the treatments and procedures I'll have to go through again, and I feel like I'm not strong enough to face them. I become anxious and depressed, and it's hard for me to find joy in anything. I start to avoid thinking about it, but then I feel guilty for not facing it head-on."

Therapist: "I understand how you're feeling. Feeling overwhelmed and helpless when faced with a challenging situation is normal. Who would you be without the belief I can't handle the cancer coming back?"

Janet: "I'm not sure. It's hard to imagine myself without that belief because it feels like such a core part of my identity right now."

Therapist: "That's understandable. It's natural to identify with our thoughts and beliefs, but it's important to remember that they are just thoughts and beliefs. Take a few moments to sit with this question and see what comes up for you."

Janet: (pause) "Without that belief, I would feel more confident and capable. I would feel more in control of my life and my treatment. I would feel like I have more options and that I can handle whatever comes my way."

Therapist: "That's great. It sounds like letting go of the belief that you can't handle the cancer coming back has allowed you to tap into your own inner strength and resilience. Are you ready to turn around the thought, "I can't handle the cancer coming back"?

Janet: "How do I do that?"

Therapist: "Try the simple opposite. What is the opposite of 'I can't'?"

Janet: "I *can* handle the cancer coming back."

Therapist: "Could you give us some specific examples of how or why you can handle the cancer coming back?"

Janet: "Well, I've been through cancer treatments before, and I know what to expect. I have a strong support system of family and friends who have been with me every step of the way. I have also learned coping skills and self-care techniques that have helped me get through the tough times. I have a strong faith and belief in myself and my ability to overcome challenges, which gives me the strength and determination to handle the cancer coming back."

Therapist: "That's great, Janet. It sounds like you have a wealth of resources and support to draw upon during this difficult time. Is there anything else you would like to work on or any other thoughts or beliefs that are causing you suffering?"

Janet: "I think I'm good for now. Thank you for guiding me through The Work and helping me see things in a different light. It's been very helpful."

Janet made remarkable progress in the following months. She developed a strong sense of self-assurance and grit, which enabled her to confront the difficulties of her cancer recurrence. She established a reliable network of support from other group members, acquired coping techniques, and developed an unwavering belief in herself that would sustain her through this challenging period.

Here is a partial list of other beliefs that came up in the group:

- I am ashamed of the "side effects" of cancer
- I can't stand the uncertainty of my future
- I am being a burden to my family
- I lack control and autonomy
- I am unable to live my life
- I don't like how people feel sorry for me
- I want to take care of people
- I am losing my privacy and identity
- Everyone has advice and a story
- Doctors leave the decision to you
- I feel blamed for having cancer

- I am scared about the effects of chemotherapy
- I hate the denial of symptoms by the medical professionals
- I am afraid of getting other cancers
- It is hard to keep up with other responsibilities in life
- I am unable to make plans
- My treatment is stressful when doctors disagree on the course
- I fear invisibility and uncertainty
- I feel blamed
- I fear the complications of the treatment itself

The Work, as we delve deeper into it, is an incisive method of self-inquiry tailored to assist those grappling with chronic pain. At its core, it prompts individuals to identify and dissect distressing thoughts or beliefs, assess their veracity, and observe their influence on emotions and behaviors. By undergoing this inquiry, individuals can confront and reevaluate negative beliefs, which often intensify their physical discomfort.

Consider this: an individual facing chronic pain might harbor the thought, "I cannot bear this pain any longer." Within the framework of The Work, they'd first scrutinize the authenticity of such a claim. Is it unequivocally true they can no longer endure the pain? What unfolds internally when they latch onto this belief? What external reactions manifest? Such probing can usher in the realization that their held belief may magnify their agony.

Subsequently, in asking question #4, they'd probe the essence of their being without this belief. This exploration paves the way for envisioning a fresh viewpoint, one where pain doesn't consume their identity. They'd reframe the belief, perhaps turning it around as "I can navigate through this pain." They'd then seek tangible instances in their life where this reframed belief resonates as truth.

Traditional talk therapy often involves a lengthy process of exploring past experiences, traumas, and subconscious motives. While this is undoubtedly valuable, The Work provides a more immediate, direct route to confronting the thoughts that exacerbate chronic pain here and now. It empowers the client to actively engage in their own healing by questioning the validity of their distressing thoughts and discovering new perspectives.

The Work, for those wrestling with chronic pain, is not just another tool—it's an empowering avenue to challenge debilitating beliefs and alleviate the intertwined emotional turmoil of physical pain. Beyond mere relief, it empowers them to reclaim agency over their healing journey, drawing from their innate reservoir of resilience and strength. This sense of agency can be incredibly liberating for those dealing with chronic pain, as it shifts the focus from passive suffering to active coping and resilience.

## REFLECTION QUESTIONS

1. How might you help a client like Janet examine her underlying beliefs and assumptions about her cancer?

2. What stood out to you from the list of beliefs expressed in the cancer support group? How might you respond compassionately while guiding inquiry with these beliefs as a therapist?

3. Janet made remarkable progress through The Work. What do you think enabled her transformation? As a therapist, how can you create conditions that allow similar breakthroughs with clients?

4. How might The Work be integrated into your therapeutic approach and framework? What opportunities and challenges do you see?

5. What resonated with you from this depiction of using The Work with cancer patients? How might you apply any insights to your own life and growth?

# CHAPTER 11

## Eating Disorders

For 18 years of my professional life, I worked in a student health center of a large public university with over 40,000 students. There were a lot of students on campus who struggled with issues about eating and body image. You have probably encountered many young women in your practice who are at risk for developing eating disorders or have already begun to develop disordered eating behavior. It is essential to be proactive in offering information and support. In my experience, the most effective interventions focus on exploring individual values and beliefs and challenging media and popular culture messages.

Here is a list of beliefs I collected while working with students diagnosed with an eating disorder:

- I must be thin and lose weight to be happy, successful, and loved.
- My worth is directly related to my appearance and how much I weigh.
- I need to diet or control my food intake in order to be healthy.
- I must exercise excessively to burn off calories and prevent weight gain.
- I am an inadequate or unworthy person if I fail to control my eating and lose weight.

- I am fat, and it is my fault.
- Thinness equals happiness, success, and being worthy of love.
- I can only be happy, successful, and loved if I am thin.
- I must be perfect in all aspects of my life, including my weight and appearance.
- If people see me as overweight or obese, they will judge me, and I will be rejected.
- Eating disorders are a way of coping with stressful situations or emotions.
- I am in control when I restrict my food intake and/or purging.
- Losing weight will make all my problems go away.
- I deserve to be punished for my bad behavior by restricting my food intake and/or purging.
- I am not good enough the way I am.

The National Eating Disorder Association (NEDA) highlights that eating disorders rank as the third most prevalent chronic illness among college students. These disorders frequently manifest during formative years—adolescence or young adulthood—with college often serving as a catalyst. Understanding the underlying factors contributing to this prevalence is crucial for therapists like you who are positioned to make a tangible impact.

College is often heralded as a time of transition, discovery, and personal growth. Students find themselves untethered from the familial nest for the first time, reveling in newfound freedoms and responsibilities. Yet, this exhilarating chapter can also be fraught with anxieties and insecurities. For some students, resorting to disordered eating becomes a maladaptive strategy to regain a semblance of control over their turbulent lives.

Another contributing factor is the immense pressure to excel academically. Students often internalize the belief that their worth is intrinsically tied to their academic performance. This unforgiving mindset can cultivate perfectionism, a well-documented precursor to eating disorders like anorexia nervosa and bulimia. While eating disorders have long been stereotypically associated with young women—with up to 15 percent of females in high school and college reported as affected—let's not overlook the male demographic. Increasingly, males, and notably gay males, are falling prey to body image issues and disordered eating behaviors.

The societal pressure to conform to an idealized thinness is gender-neutral. We live in a culture that disproportionately values appearance over character or abilities, propagating the "thin ideal" as a universal standard of beauty. This cultural narrative varies from beliefs like, "If I'm thin, I'll be more accepted," to "Being slim is attractive," and even "I must be skinny for people to like me." The internalization of these messages can propel individuals into a dangerous cycle of food restriction, excessive exercise, and extreme dieting, setting the stage for eating disorders.

Beyond the obvious physical health repercussions, individuals embroiled in this vicious cycle often battle a host of mental health issues. Anxiety, depression, social withdrawal, and plummeting self-esteem are frequently comorbid with disordered eating behaviors. Alarmingly, many individuals languish undiagnosed until their condition becomes severe, a status quo maintained by societal stigma around mental health treatment and a widespread lack of education on the early warning signs of eating disorders.

The emotional toll of an eating disorder cannot be overstated. Afflicted individuals often find themselves on a destructive path, weighed down by guilt and confusion, all while striving to meet weight loss goals that they have either consciously or subconsciously internalized due to societal pressures.

Now, let's delve into how negative beliefs can lead to the development of an eating disorder in a clinical setting. Jane was a client who had embraced a number of these beliefs. When she came to see me, she was an 18-year-old freshman who had a lot of negative beliefs about her body and her self-worth. She believed she had to be thin to be worthy of love and success and thought she had to control her food intake strictly to stay healthy. These all-or-nothing beliefs were so entrenched in Jane's mind that she developed an eating disorder as a result. As time passed, Jane began to believe that to be loved and successful, she had to be thin at all costs. Her eating habits became increasingly extreme as she desperately tried to control her eating and weight. She eliminated entire food groups from her diet until only a few items remained that she would allow herself to eat.

When Jane came for help at the clinic, it quickly became apparent that these negative beliefs had taken such a strong hold over her life that they had caused an eating disorder that required immediate attention and treatment.

I introduced Jane to the *Judge-Your-Body Worksheet* developed by Byron Katie—see the end of this chapter. Here is what Jane wrote on the Worksheet:

- I am disgusted with my body because it is so fat and ugly.
- I want my body to be thin and beautiful.
- My body should be more flexible. It should not put on extra weight on my hips and thighs.
- I need my body to stay fit and light.
- My body is weak, bloated, ugly, and distorted.
- I don't ever want to be ashamed of my body in public. I don't ever want to feel inadequate because of my fat body.

I guided her through the four questions and the turnarounds on her negative beliefs about her body, which she captured using the Worksheet. We began by doing The Work on her belief: "My body is too fat and ugly." Here is a partial transcript of the inquiry with Jane. At first, Jane was resistant to challenging those beliefs. She felt it would be too hard or uncomfortable or that it wouldn't even make a difference anyway.

Therapist: "Jane, your body is too fat and ugly—is that true?"
Jane: "Yes."
Therapist: "Can you absolutely know that it is true?"
Jane: "Yes."
Therapist: "How do you react, what happens, when you believe your body is too fat and ugly?"
Jane: "I feel inadequate, ashamed, and frustrated when I have that thought. I hide from public events, especially those that include eating in front of others. I wear baggy clothes. I hate myself and feel unworthy. I envy my friends who are outgoing and relaxed. I think everyone judges me harshly because of my appearance."
Therapist: "I can see how that must be hard for you. Who would you be without that thought?"
Jane: "I would be more accepting of myself and my body. I would be more compassionate toward myself. I would feel more confident and at ease around food. I would be free."
Therapist: "Notice how you feel and react with and without the belief your body is too fat and ugly. Are you ready to turn that thought around?"
Jane: "My body is not too fat and ugly."

Therapist: "Yes, your body is good enough just as it is. Now see if you can come up with a couple of specific examples of the turnaround."

Jane: "I am fit enough to be on the basketball team. (Smiling) My boyfriend says he loves me just the way I am."

Although Jane struggled with her eating disorder for some time after beginning The Work, she eventually developed healthier thinking patterns about herself and food. Instead of focusing on deprivation or punishment for what she ate, she started viewing food as nourishment and enjoyment. This allowed Jane more freedom from the rigidity of her old belief system; instead of feeling like every decision around food was life or death, it became more manageable and could even be enjoyed in moderation.

Additionally, by engaging with The Work regularly, Jane was also able to challenge many of the underlying beliefs she had about herself: that she wasn't worthy unless she was thin, that without rigid control over what she ate, nothing good could follow, etc. As these core beliefs shifted through the process of The Work, so did Jane's attitude towards food, eventually becoming one grounded in pleasure rather than punishment.

Although challenging at times along the way—shifting long-held negative beliefs can often feel overwhelming—Jane's journey toward recovery is ultimately one filled with hope: hope for a brighter future where worthiness isn't based on appearance and health isn't limited by restriction but can instead be celebrated through balance and joyfulness. She started having fun with the process and allowing herself more flexibility with her thinking around food, self-image, and worthiness.

The Work can be effective in dealing with eating disorders when the individual is open to challenging their deeply ingrained beliefs about their body and self-worth. Signs of progress may include the individual's willingness to engage in the process, ability to identify and question their negative beliefs, and capacity to develop healthier thinking patterns about themselves and food.

However, there are red flags that therapists should be aware of that suggest the person with the eating disorder is in danger and needs inpatient care. These may include extreme weight loss, severe restriction of food intake, frequent purging behaviors, and signs of malnutrition such as dizziness, fainting, or irregular heart rhythms.

Furthermore, suppose the individual's negative beliefs about their body and self-worth are so entrenched that they resist challenging them, as was initially the case with Jane. This may also be a sign that more intensive treatment is needed in that case.

In such cases, therapists must be proactive in offering information and support and consider referring the individual to a specialized eating disorder treatment program.

THE WORK of Byron Katie®

# Judge-Your-Body Worksheet

**Judge your body • Write it down • Ask four questions • Turn it around**

**Think of a recurring stressful thought about your body or a part of your body. (You may replace the word "body" in the questions and answers below with "legs," "belly," "heart," "cancer," etc.)**

1. **What is it about your body that angers, confuses, or disappoints you, and why?**

   I am ____________ at my body because ____________________________________________
   *emotion*

   ______________________________________________________________________

   *Example:* I am *angry* at my body because *it is old.*

2. **How do you want your body to change?**

   I want my body to ____________________________________________________________

   ______________________________________________________________________

   ______________________________________________________________________

   *Example:* I want my body to *be young and free of wrinkles. I want my body to lose weight.*

3. **What advice would you offer to your body?**

   My body should/shouldn't ______________________________________________________

   ______________________________________________________________________

   ______________________________________________________________________

   ______________________________________________________________________

   *Example:* My body should *stop getting old. My body should be pain free.*

4. **In order for you to be happy, what do you need your body to be or do?**

   I need my body to ____________________________________________________________

   ______________________________________________________________________

   ______________________________________________________________________

   *Example:* I need my body to *stay beautiful forever. I need my body to attract a lover. I need my body to stay young.*

5. **What do you think of your body? Make a list.**

   My body is _________________________________________________________________

   ______________________________________________________________________

   *Example:* My body is *ugly, wrinkled all over, disgusting, inflexible, in pain, and out of control.*

6. **What is it in or about your body that you don't ever want to experience again?**

   I don't ever want ____________________________________________________________

   ______________________________________________________________________

   ______________________________________________________________________

   *Example:* I don't ever want *people to see me as too fat again. I don't ever want my body to be in pain again.*

**For more information on how to do The Work, visit www.thework.com**

# REFLECTION QUESTIONS

1. What beliefs do you notice your clients struggling with related to their bodies, food, or self-worth? How might you help them investigate those beliefs more deeply?

2. Do any of the example beliefs from the students in this chapter resonate with clients you have worked with? What was similar or different about their experiences?

3. How might you use the Judge-Your-Body Worksheet to explore eating disorder beliefs with your clients?

4. How did this chapter affect your views on addressing eating disorders through exploring underlying beliefs? Were any of your previous assumptions challenged?

5. What stood out to you most in Jane's journey of using The Work to address her eating disorder? How might you apply insights from her case to your clients?

# CHAPTER 12

## Procrastination and Perfectionism

You have probably had to deal with many clients who come to you for help with procrastination. This can be a challenging group to work with, but by using The Work, they can make significant progress. For over ten years, I ran multiple groups for students struggling with procrastination and perfectionism. The problem of procrastination is not limited to college students. You may have encountered people with procrastination from all age groups and socio-economic backgrounds in your work.

People procrastinate for many reasons, but some of the most common beliefs contributing to this behavior are perfectionism, fear of failure, and low self-confidence.

Perfectionism is the belief that everything must be done perfectly to succeed. This can lead to procrastination because people may feel like they can't start something unless they know they can do it perfectly, which is often impossible.

Perfectionism and Imposter Syndrome usually go hand in hand with Procrastination. Over the years, I noticed recurring beliefs among the participants. Here are some beliefs that can lead to procrastination, as gathered from our groups:

- Everything must be done perfectly to be successful.
- I'm not good enough, so why bother trying?
- I don't have time to do it right now.
- It's too difficult.
- I'll do it later when I'm in the mood.
- I don't know how to do it.
- I'm afraid of failing.
- Someone else can do it better than me.

It's incredible to witness the transformation in the group as the diehard procrastinators start to question their assumptions. The room fills with laughter and a newfound sense of lightness as they begin to see the truth in the opposite of their long-held beliefs.

When clients come to therapy feeling stuck and unsure about a decision, I often turn to the Decision Matrix. It's a simple but powerful tool. I ask them to get a pen and paper and list their hopes and fears for each potential choice. You'd be amazed at how often this alone can bring clarity. There's something about getting it all out on paper that helps us see things in a new light.

But sometimes, even after they've poured their hearts out onto the page, they still feel paralyzed. That's when I invite them to take a closer look at their list of fears. We dive in together, using The Work to challenge and question those fears one by one. It's fascinating to watch as their perspective shifts and those once-daunting fears start to lose their power.

On the other hand, we usually leave their list of hopes untouched. They're not the ones causing stress or holding them back. By the time we've worked through the fears, the decision often becomes crystal clear. It's like a weight has been lifted, and they can finally move forward with confidence and peace of mind.

Here is an example of a decision matrix completed by a 35-year-old Jewish man trying to decide whether to stay married or separate from his wife of six years.

| Hopes | Fears |
|---|---|
| **Decision #1: Stay Married** | |
| Have a family together. | She doesn't grow in the ways I need her to. |
| Grow old together. | I feel trapped. |
| Learn and love with each other. | We end up breaking up later. |
| Push each other to achieve our goals. | She doesn't fully understand me. |
| Overcome insecurities. | We can't agree on anything. |
| **Decision #2: We Separate** | |
| Find someone with shared beliefs and interests. | I or she will be heart-broken. |
| I learn more about myself and my interests. | I will miss her more than it's worth. |
| I will grow stronger. | Life will change for the worse. |
| I will grow more independent. | I'll realize I want to be with her. |

Our role as a therapist is to guide clients through the complexities of their inner world, particularly when it comes to behaviors that undermine their success, such as procrastination. We can empower them by helping them uncover and examine the fears and beliefs that propel their avoidance. Utilize practical tools, like the Decision Matrix discussed earlier, to assist clients in delineating their hopes and apprehensions regarding each decision. This isn't merely illuminating; it gives them the necessary clarity and focus to confront their fears directly.

Nevertheless, remain vigilant for red flags. Persistent negative self-beliefs—statements like "I'm not good enough, so why bother?" "I'm afraid of failing" or "Someone else can do it better"—are not just passing thoughts. They are symptomatic of deeper emotional struggles such as low self-esteem, fear of failure, or entrenched perfectionism. These issues might require a more sophisticated therapeutic strategy.

Moreover, scrutinize the fears your client records in the Decision Matrix. If these fears are substantial and associated with detrimental behaviors, it indicates that the client may benefit from more intensive assistance. For example, suppose a client's fear of remaining in a marriage is linked to feelings of entrapment or persistent conflict. In that case, you've pinpointed relational problems that could be more effectively addressed through couples therapy or similar specialized approaches.

# REFLECTION QUESTIONS

1. As a therapist, what beliefs do you commonly encounter in your clients that contribute to procrastination? How could you use The Work to help them investigate these beliefs?

2. Have you witnessed a client make a decision after listing out their hopes and fears for each option? What was that process like for them? How did writing out their thoughts help lead them to a decision?

3. What fears or concerns come up for you around using The Work with clients struggling with procrastination or difficult decisions? How might you address those concerns?

4. How could you adapt the decision matrix example in this chapter for other types of decisions your clients are facing (career choices, relationship issues, etc.)?

# CHAPTER 13

## Suicide and Depression

In the realm of psychotherapy, you're no stranger to the profound emotional pain that clients struggling with depression and suicidal ideation experience. The undercurrent of negative core beliefs—such as worthlessness, shame, guilt, hopelessness, and helplessness—can be both debilitating and complex. Among these, the feeling of being irrevocably trapped often propels individuals toward considering suicide as an escape route. This drastic choice is usually perceived as a permanent solution to what are, in most cases, temporary problems.

Understanding the genesis of these core negative beliefs is critical for effective therapeutic intervention. Let's delve into some of the key contributing factors.

Adverse Childhood Experiences (ACEs) are a potent incubator for negative core beliefs. Emotional, physical, and sexual abuse, as well as neglect, can inflict lasting psychological scars that manifest as self-loathing, guilt, and an entrenched feeling of inadequacy. These early traumas don't merely fade away with time; they often lay the foundation for persistent negative thought patterns that fuel depression and suicidal ideation.

The role of genetics and familial mental health shouldn't be underestimated. Often, these negative core beliefs can be part of a complex intergenerational cycle of mental health issues. Certain genetic predispositions may make individuals more susceptible to developing these beliefs. Recent studies have identified specific DNA variants associated with the risk of attempting suicide. For instance, a large study found 12 DNA variants linked to suicide attempt risk. (Jones, 2023) When you combine genetic vulnerabilities with a family environment that may inadvertently reinforce negative self-concepts, the risk of developing depression and suicidal thoughts increases substantially.

Let's also consider the role of specific life events outside of childhood. Events such as a painful breakup, the loss of a loved one, or a career setback can act as triggers for those already predisposed to negative thinking. While these experiences are not necessarily traumatic in the traditional sense, they can still catalyze the formation or reinforcement of negative core beliefs, particularly in individuals with a pre-existing propensity for such thought patterns.

Therapists face the challenge of untangling this complex web of factors to identify the most effective treatment approach. Techniques like cognitive behavioral therapy (CBT) are often effective in challenging and reframing negative core beliefs. However, for clients with histories of trauma, additional trauma-informed care or even dialectical behavior therapy (DBT) may be more appropriate.

Incorporating methods like The Work of Byron Katie can offer another layer of transformative potential. By questioning the validity of these deeply ingrained negative beliefs and examining them from multiple perspectives, clients can gain a newfound awareness and potentially break free from the self-imposed mental traps.

Your expertise places you in a unique position to effect change. By gaining a deep understanding of the origins and perpetuation of negative core beliefs, you can tailor your therapeutic strategies to not only mitigate the symptoms of depression and suicidal ideation but also empower your clients to challenge and alter these destructive beliefs. This is where you can turn the temporary into the transitional, guiding your clients away from a precipice and toward a life of greater emotional freedom and well-being. Let's consider a clinical example.

It was Rakesh's difficult childhood experiences with his mother that led him to my office. Like many individuals, Rakesh's negative beliefs about himself and his worth were formed early on and reinforced through years of strained relationships with close family members. These beliefs can be especially detrimental when they are left unexamined and unchallenged, leading to the development of mental health issues like depression and suicidal ideation.

Rakesh had been dreading this time of year for a long time. As a 40-year-old realtor, he was used to traveling, but the thought of going home to his mother's house made him anxious. Rakesh and his mother had been at odds over his career choices and future plans for years. His mother was deeply disappointed when Rakesh decided not to pursue his dream of becoming a doctor as she had always hoped. From then on, their relationship became strained and marked by tension and judgment.

Whenever they talked, Rakesh felt like nothing he could do or say would ever be enough to make her proud again. Their conversations were characterized by awkward silences and harsh words, sometimes ending in angry arguments that left Rakesh feeling helpless and ashamed. He often felt like she was constantly looking over his shoulder, waiting for him to fail so she could point out how much better things would have been if only he had listened to her from the start.

Rakesh knew that going home for the holidays would mean facing all these difficult emotions head-on, and he couldn't bring himself to do it anymore. He decided instead to stay alone in his own city, far from his mother's, and take a break from the constant judgment he received from her every time they were together. However, the last time he stayed alone in his apartment during the holidays, he had intentionally overdosed on alcohol and a cocktail of prescription pills that were in his bathroom cabinet. He was lucky that time that he had a concerned neighbor who checked on him using the spare key he had given her. Since Rakesh has made some progress since his suicide attempt, I decided it was time for him to question his assumptions about his mother and not hide from her this year.

Here is his Judge-Your-Neighbor Worksheet on his mother:

- I am feeling bitter toward Mom because she passes judgment on me without questioning it.
- I want her to stop judging me. I want her to accept me for who I am and not what she wants me to be.
- She should drop her unsubstantiated assumptions about me. She should accept that people can have different views and not be evil or bad.
- I need her to be chill like my friends.
- She is opinionated, stubborn, lazy, and not responsible.
- I don't want her to pass judgment on me.

We did the inquiry on "she passes judgment on me." Here is an abbreviated version of the session with Rakesh:

Therapist: "Good afternoon, Rakesh. How are you feeling today?"

Rakesh: "To be honest, not great. I had another argument with my Mom and it's really weighing on me."

Therapist: "I'm sorry to hear that. Would you like to work through these feelings today?"

Rakesh: "Yes, that's why I'm here."

Therapist: "Great. Let's start by identifying a specific belief about your mother that's causing you stress."

Rakesh: "Well, I believe she passes judgment on me all the time."

Therapist: "Alright, let's work with that. The first question is: Is it true?"

Rakesh: "Yes."

Therapist: "Can you absolutely know that it's true that she passes judgment on you?"

Rakesh: "Hmm, when you put it that way... I can't say it's "absolutely" true. Maybe I'm interpreting her actions as judgmental."

Therapist: "Interesting insight. Let's move on to the third question: How do you react when you believe your mother is passing judgment on you?"

Rakesh: "When I believe she's judging me, I feel this rush of emotions—anger, defensiveness, and shame. My first instinct is to lash out, to confront her. Sometimes, I do end up saying things I later regret. It's like I'm trying to protect myself, but I end up causing more harm.

I also find myself avoiding deeper conversations with her, sticking to superficial topics to sidestep the possibility of feeling judged. It's as if this invisible barrier keeps me from being fully present or vulnerable around her.

Even when she's talking about something unrelated, I'm on high alert, scanning for any signs of judgment or criticism. This means I'm not really listening to her; I'm listening to my own internal narrative about what she might be thinking.

And then there's the emotional toll. I find myself ruminating over our interactions, replaying conversations in my head, and imagining different outcomes where I stand up to her judgment. But these are just fantasies; they don't resolve anything.

When I'm caught in this belief, I realize I'm not just distancing myself from her emotionally; I'm also shutting down avenues for understanding or reconciliation. I become so focused on defending myself that I can't see her perspective or consider that maybe she's coming from a place of concern or love, however misguided it might be.

This belief that she's judging me paralyzes our relationship. It prevents me from taking steps that could improve our interaction, like asking her what she really meant or expressing how her words made me feel. I'm so preoccupied with my own defensive stance that I miss the opportunity for a genuine connection."

Therapist: "Who would you be without the thought?"

Rakesh: "I guess I'd be more open to understanding her point of view rather than just shutting down the conversation. Without this belief that she's constantly judging me, I can see myself as being more relaxed and present when I'm around her. There's an openness, a kind of emotional spaciousness that allows for more genuine interaction. I think I'd actually listen to what she's saying rather than scanning her words for hidden judgments. I'd probably be more compassionate, too. I could consider her point of view, understanding that she might have her own fears and insecurities that influence how she interacts with me. Rather than jumping to conclusions, I'd give her the benefit of the doubt more often.

Without that defensive barrier, I can see myself opening up to her in ways that I haven't before. We could discuss deeper topics, share more about our lives, and maybe even resolve some of the lingering issues that have been left unspoken. I'd be more inclined to ask her about her feelings and thoughts, creating a two-way dialogue instead of a one-sided defense.

I'd probably feel more empowered to express my boundaries and needs in a clear, assertive way—instead of a reactive one. I could say, "Mom, when you say things like that, it makes me feel judged," and it would come from a place of wanting to improve the relationship, not just fend off an attack.

Emotionally, I think I'd feel lighter, less burdened. It's exhausting to always be on the defensive, to carry that emotional armor around all the time. Without this belief, I imagine there'd be a greater sense of freedom and ease, not just with her but in other relationships."

Therapist: "Now for the turnarounds. Let's begin by stating the opposite of your original belief and then finding at least three genuine examples of how the turnaround is true."

Rakesh: "The opposite of "My mother passes judgment on me" could be "My mother does not pass judgment on me.""

Therapist: "Can you find three instances where this is true?"

Rakesh: "This is tough, but let me try. Ultimately, she was supportive when I changed my career path, even though it was hard for her. Second, she often says she just wants me to be happy. Third, when I think about it, she does listen when I explain my point of view; maybe I just felt judged because I was already defensive."

Therapist: "Let's consider another turnaround. Can you turn it around to your mother?"

Rakesh: "I pass judgment on my mother?"

Therapist: "Yes. Can you find at least three examples where this might be true?"

Rakesh: "That's a bit uncomfortable to think about, but yes, I can see it. First, I often criticize her in my mind for being too controlling. Second, I judge her for not understanding me or my choices. And third, I sometimes look down on her for not being as open-minded as I'd like her to be."

Therapist: "How does acknowledging these judgments change your perspective on the original belief?"

Rakesh: "It's kind of humbling. I realize I'm doing the same thing I accuse her of doing. It makes me wonder if my judgment towards her is a defense mechanism to shield myself from feeling judged."

Therapist: "Good. Now, can you turn the thought to yourself?"

Rakesh: "I pass judgment on myself."

Therapist: "Excellent, Rakesh. Can you think of three examples where this has been true?"

Rakesh: "Wow, this one hits close to home. First, I judge myself for not meeting my high standards, whether at work or in my personal life. Second, I criticize myself for being unable to handle criticism ironically. And third, I often feel like I'm not living up to the expectations I assume others have for me, even when those expectations are just in my head."

Therapist: "How does recognizing these self-judgments influence your view of the original issue?"

Rakesh: "It's eye-opening. I see now that a lot of the judgment I felt from my mother might actually be a projection of my self-judgment. Maybe I've been so focused on external judgments because it's easier than facing my inner critic."

Therapist: "Excellent work, Rakesh. How do you feel now that you've gone through this process?"

Rakesh: "Lighter. It's like I've been carrying this weight of judgment, and now it feels less heavy."

Therapist: "That's the power of The Work. It's a tool you can use whenever you struggle with stressful beliefs. How does this experience make you feel about addressing issues with your mother going forward?"

Rakesh: "More hopeful, definitely. And equipped with a new way to approach our relationship."

Therapist: "Wonderful. Remember, The Work is a practice, not a one-time fix. But it's a valuable technique for reframing the beliefs that cause you stress."

Rakesh: "Absolutely. Thank you for introducing me to this."

By guiding your clients through The Work, you've offered them immediate relief and equipped them with a tool for lifelong self-inquiry and personal growth. This kind of transformative psychotherapy can evolve as a practice and deeply enrich your clients' lives.

Rakesh could see how his judgments of himself were far worse than his mother's. We also did the "prescription for happiness" technique, turning around his answers to questions number two, three, and four:

- I want to stop judging myself. I want to accept myself for who I am and not what my Mom wants me to be.

- I should drop my unsubstantiated assumptions about myself (and her). I should accept that people can have different views and not be evil or bad.
- I need me to be chill like my friends (around their Moms).

Rakesh was stunned to realize how much he lived under the dark shadows of his assumptions and beliefs about himself and his Mom. Through our work together using The Work, Rakesh could question his assumptions and beliefs, leading to a greater sense of self-acceptance and a more positive relationship with his mother. Thus, instead of remaining home and alone over the holidays, he decided to visit her during the holiday season, and they had a wonderful time together.

The effectiveness of The Work in dealing with suicide and depression can be gauged by observing changes in the clients' negative beliefs and assumptions about themselves and others. As your client begins questioning these beliefs and assumptions, they may experience greater self-acceptance and improved relationships, as with Rakesh.

However, the therapist must remain vigilant for any red flags that suggest your client may be in danger. These could include expressions of feelings of increasing anxiety, anger, worthlessness, shame, guilt, hopelessness, helplessness, and the feeling of being trapped. If your client has a history of suicide attempts, like Rakesh, this should also be taken into account.

In such cases, you should consider whether your client needs additional help, such as more intensive therapy or medical intervention. It is important to remember that while The Work can be a powerful tool in addressing negative beliefs and assumptions, it may not be sufficient on its own for clients who are at high risk of suicide or are severely depressed.

## REFLECTION QUESTIONS

1. How might you help a client like Rakesh examine his underlying assumptions about himself and his mother?

2. When working with suicidal clients, how can you compassionately challenge their negative beliefs while also ensuring their safety? What precautions or resources might you put in place?

3. What childhood experiences or family dynamics have you commonly seen underlying suicidal ideation or depression in your clients? How might you adapt The Work to address these root causes?

4. Rakesh's strained relationship with his mother contributed to his depression. How could family counseling or involving loved ones in The Work benefit clients like Rakesh? What challenges might this present?

5. How might you adapt the techniques in this chapter to work with depressed or suicidal clients who have different presenting problems than Rakesh? Are there any limitations of The Work you foresee?

# CHAPTER 14

## Prejudice

One of the most challenging issues therapists face today is helping clients navigate the emotional and psychological stressors caused by the increasing polarization in society. Whether it manifests as family discord, social anxiety, or a sense of existential dread, the impact of this divisive climate frequently becomes a focal point of therapy sessions. But how do you effectively address these stressors without introducing your own biases into the therapeutic space?

So, here's a question to ponder: What if you could provide a robust framework that empowers your clients to confront their biases and engage in meaningful dialogue, all while maintaining the crucial therapeutic principle of neutrality?

As psychotherapists, we are supposed to be neutral. We are taught not to judge our clients and instead focus on helping them find the answers to their problems. We must also be aware of our biases, preconceptions, and expectations. We must recognize that we are not experts on our clients' lives, beliefs, or experiences. We should respect their autonomy and be open to learning from them.

Meanwhile, political, racial, and economic polarization worldwide has been rising for some years now. Much of this can be attributed to prejudice and the reinforcement of negative stereotypes. Bias is often created out of fear or misinformation, which leads to skewed perceptions that are hard to overcome. Polarization only divides us further, leading to an atmosphere of distrust and misunderstanding among different groups. We must recognize and confront our personal biases and closely held beliefs to work towards unifying an increasingly polarized world.

As therapists, we have an essential responsibility to help our clients cope with the effects of political polarization. To ensure we can assist our clients in the most effective way possible, it is crucial to understand the root causes of polarization in ourselves and our clients. We can provide a safe and non-judgmental environment for clients to understand their emotions and thoughts related to political issues. Furthermore, we can provide various tools and strategies to encourage effective communication and dialogue between individuals with different political views and to help individuals understand how their biases can affect their opinions. (Guzmán, M. 2022). Lastly, we can also use The Work to help our clients explore their biases and outlooks and learn to effectively communicate and respectfully engage with those who disagree with them. By understanding the affects of polarization and providing the necessary tools and strategies, we can help individuals create productive dialogue and reduce political polarization.

I have a personal story that I wanted to add here. In the early 2000s, I attended a residential seminar in Southern California held at a golf course in a predominantly Republican county. At the time, George Bush had just become president after a fiercely contested Supreme Court battle, and I held strong negative feelings towards Republicans. One day during the seminar, we were addressing prejudice, and I filled out a Judge-Your-Neighbor Worksheet with all my negative thoughts about Republicans.

At the end of the day, the seminar leader asked us to dress up and play the part of whoever we were prejudiced against. I was stumped when it came to figuring out how Republicans dress, so I asked a friend for help. She pointed at me and said, "Like this," which we both found hilarious. She even gave me a bag of her golf clubs, and my roommate lent me a polo shirt and a golf cap.

To my surprise, the golfers at the course were incredibly friendly to me, striking up conversations and treating me with respect. This experience was eye-opening, and it made me realize that we are not our beliefs. Our opinions and judgments of others can be based on stereotypes and assumptions that are not necessarily true.

Overall, this experience was a valuable lesson in recognizing and challenging my prejudices and beliefs. It showed me the importance of keeping an open mind and stepping outside my comfort zone to understand others truly.

The Work serves as a potent medium for therapists to guide clients, whether it's a client expressing racist views or someone facing prejudice, in introspecting their thoughts and beliefs. Take a MAGA supporter with the belief that "Democrats are wreaking havoc on the country." Through The Work, a therapist can steer them toward questioning the authenticity and implications of such a viewpoint.

Possible turnarounds might challenge the supporter to identify ways in which the contrary perspective might be equally or more valid. For instance, how might Democrats be aiding the country, or could Republicans, in specific ways, also be contributing to challenges faced by the nation? This introspection can unveil biases and illustrate how these predispositions mold their viewpoints and color their interactions.

Conversely, for someone bearing the brunt of prejudice, The Work becomes an avenue to navigate the emotional turbulence stemming from discrimination and to address any self-deprecating beliefs. Let's say a client is entrenched in the thought, "My worth is diminished due to my racial background." The therapist can utilize The Work to prod this belief, dissecting its origins and bearing on their self-worth and interpersonal dynamics.

Whether aiding a political supporter or someone combating prejudice, the therapist's paramount responsibility is to carve out a sanctuary—free from judgments—enabling your client to delve deep into their emotions and thoughts. Beyond mere introspection, therapists equip clients with effective communication tools, ensuring their interactions remain considerate and respectful in diverse situations.

I would like to end this chapter by giving you an edited version of a session I had with Emily many years ago. Emily was in her mid-twenties. She was born and raised in a rich, White suburban community in Southern California. Here is a summary of my session with her:

Therapist: "Good afternoon, Emily. How are you today?"

Emily: "I'm okay, I guess. I have just been feeling anxious about everything happening in the world and on campus."

Therapist: "I hear you. It's a challenging time. What specifically has been bothering you?"

Emily: "Well, there's a lot of talk about social justice, privilege, and race these days. I feel like I'm always walking on eggshells, afraid I'll say the wrong thing."

Therapist: "Sounds stressful. Want to dig into that a bit more?"

Emily: "Sure, it's just...I grew up in a primarily white, affluent area. I wasn't exposed to much diversity, and now I feel like I'm always making judgments about people based on where they're from or what they look like. And it makes me uncomfortable."

Therapist: "Thank you for sharing that, Emily. Would you like to explore these judgments through The Work?"

Emily: "Okay, let's try it."

Therapist: "Great, let's start by identifying a specific thought you've had that you find troubling."

Emily: "Um, okay. Sometimes, I think people from poorer backgrounds aren't as hardworking as I am."

Therapist: "Alright, let's question that thought. Is it true?"

Emily: "No."

Therapist: "How do you react, what happens, when you believe people from poorer backgrounds aren't as hardworking as you are?"

Emily: "When I believe that thought, I notice I get a mixed bag of emotions. I feel superior, like I've earned my place here, and they haven't. There's a certain pride, but it's tainted. Almost immediately, guilt follows because I know it's not fair to think that way. My chest tightens with that guilt, and it's uncomfortable.

Physically, I've noticed I might stand a bit taller and sort of puff up when I'm around students I know who come from less privileged backgrounds. It's like I'm trying to make myself bigger and more important somehow."

Therapist: "How does this thought affect your interactions with those students?"

Emily: "Honestly, it's damaging. I catch myself not wanting to work with them on group projects or study together. I feel they won't contribute as much, which I recognize is a terrible assumption. It's like I'm writing them off before giving them a chance, and that's just not fair."

Therapist: "What are you unable to do when you're under the influence of this thought?"

Emily: "I can't connect, not genuinely. I can't see them for who they are—just individuals trying to make it, like me. Instead, I see them through this filter of judgment, and it limits my ability to engage. I miss out on potentially enriching relationships, diverse perspectives, and even friendships. I also can't be the kind of person I want to be—one who's fair, compassionate, and open-minded."

Therapist: "And who would you be without this thought?"

Emily: "Without this thought, I'd be freer. I'd be more open to people, and I think I'd feel a sense of relief. I'd be more approachable and less tense, both mentally and physically. There would be a lightness in my chest instead of that tightness. I could engage with people based on their identity, not where they come from. And I think that would make me a better student, a better future professional, and honestly, a better human being. I'd probably be more open and less judgmental. Maybe even more compassionate."

Therapist: "Lastly, can you turn the thought around and find an opposite that's as true as or truer than the original thought?"

Emily: "People from poorer backgrounds can be as hardworking as I am, maybe even more so because they've had to overcome more obstacles."

Therapist: "That's a powerful turnaround. Can you think of three examples that support this new thought?"

Emily: "Well, first, there's Maria in my economics class. She's on a full scholarship and works part-time to support herself. She's always prepared for class and contributes insightful comments. She's clearly putting in the work, both academically and in her personal life."

Therapist: "That's a great example. What's the second one?"

Emily: "Second, there's James, a friend of a friend. He grew up in a low-income neighborhood and has had to work twice as hard to get to the same place. He tutors other students in math and is active in community service. His work ethic is solid; he's constantly juggling multiple responsibilities and excelling at them."

Therapist: "Excellent. Do you have a third example?"

Emily: "Yes, my roommate last year, Sarah. She was the first in her family to go to college and took out loans to be here. She would stay up late studying and help her family financially by doing freelance graphic design work. She was balancing so much, and her drive was inspiring."

Therapist: "How does it feel to recognize these examples?"

Emily: "It's humbling. It makes me realize how narrow my original thought was. These people aren't just as hardworking as me; in many ways, they're more so. And they've done it against greater odds."

Therapist: "Great, you've done well with that first turnaround. Now, let's explore some other possible turnarounds to your original thought."

Emily: "People from more affluent backgrounds are not as hardworking as I am."

Therapist: "Can you think of examples that support this turnaround?"

Emily: "Hmm, that's interesting. Yeah, I can think of a couple. First, there's Mark, a guy in my class who comes from a wealthy family. He seems to rely a lot on his parents' connections and doesn't put much effort into his studies. He even joked once about how he doesn't need to work hard because he has a job waiting for him in his dad's company."

Therapist: "Good example. And another?"

Emily: "Second, there's my cousin Lisa. She's always lived in luxury and has no job or responsibilities. She's in school but often skips classes and doesn't seem to care much about her education. It feels like she's just going through the motions because she's expected to, not because she's committed to working hard."

Therapist: "Excellent. Now, let's try another turnaround."

Emily: "I am not as hardworking as others from poorer neighborhoods."

Therapist: "Yes, good. Do any examples come to mind?"

Emily: "Wow, that hits home. It is embarrassing to admit this. I have been slacking off or procrastinating about my sociology assignments."

Therapist: "And a second example?"

Emily: "Do I have to give another example? I have trouble getting up in the morning and have missed some classes lately."

Therapist: "Good work, Emily. I appreciate your honesty and courage."

Emily: "Can I ask you something? What made you think you could help me? You were born and raised in India."

Therapist: "That's a valid question, Emily. My background differs from yours, but the beauty of The Work is that it's a universal tool for self-inquiry. It doesn't matter where I'm from or where you're from; what matters is your willingness to examine your own thoughts and beliefs. The Work provides a neutral ground where we can stand, irrespective of our backgrounds. Would you agree that today's session was beneficial in challenging your thoughts?"

Emily: "Yes, it was. I never thought about it that way."

Therapist: "The goal is to facilitate self-discovery, no matter who you are or where you come from."

The session concludes, leaving Emily with a new perspective on her prejudices and the universality of the self-inquiry tools. The Work has again proven its efficacy, transcending cultural and personal barriers.

Now that we've covered the foundations, our next chapter addresses doing The Work with care and wisdom. Facilitating deep inquiry in a clinical setting calls for sensitivity and discernment. In the next chapter, I offer insights on safely guiding your clients to their most profound truths, so get ready to integrate this powerful method into your practice with skill and compassion.

## REFLECTION QUESTIONS

1. As you read this chapter, did any personal biases or preconceptions come to mind? If so, how might you go about unpacking those thoughtfully?

2. Think of a client you currently work with who has different political views or life experiences than you. How might this chapter guide you to be more open and understanding when working with them?

3. When have you had an experience that challenged a previously held bias or assumption? What did you learn from that experience, and how might you apply what you learned to your practice?

4. What steps can you take as a therapist to create a safe space for clients to explore issues related to polarization? How might you guide them toward openness and understanding?

5. How can you use the lessons from this chapter and the author's personal story to be more aware of your biases and prejudices? What practices might help you continually reflect on blindspots?

# PART IV

# CHAPTER 15

## Going Deeper in The Work

Are you hungry for more? In this chapter, we delve into the nuanced intricacies of guiding a client to deeper layers of self-understanding. We explore a range of strategies aimed at fostering deeper introspection, ensuring each session resonates with significance and depth. Additionally, the chapter sheds light on how therapists can navigate situations where clients present factual and verifiable statements, emphasizing the delicate balance of acknowledging truth while promoting self-exploration and healing.

Imagine you are working with a client who was physically abused by their father. In response to the first question on the Judge-Your-Neighbor Worksheet, they wrote: "I am angry with my father because he beat me." When you ask the first two questions (Is it true? and Can you absolutely know that it's true?), the answer will inevitably be "yes." Of course, you can proceed to question #3 (How do you react, what happens, when you believe that thought?). However, either your client or you may feel somewhat stuck. When you or your client are stuck in your inquiry and unable to progress more deeply, try these strategies instead. They can help unlock a new perspective on something that seems like an irrefutable fact, allowing for a more productive exploration of ideas.

A powerful technique for going deeper in the inquiry process is to use the phrase "and that means that" when your client answers "yes" to questions 1 and 2. This phrase helps you both to identify the underlying interpretations and assumptions that may be causing the real suffering. In the above example, if your client finds himself feeling angry at his father because he hit him when he was a child, he might re-write the initial statement: "I am angry with my father because he hit me, and that means that he doesn't love me." By adding this phrase, you are able to identify the interpretation that his dad hitting him is a sign that he doesn't love him. So, doing an inquiry on the new statement: "My dad doesn't love me," may be more powerful and produce better results.

On some occasions, a client may believe that if an important person in their life did something, they would be happier, but they may not be consciously aware of the real reason why they are upset. For example, the initial statement might be, "My boss didn't give me a raise in my salary this year." So when your client answers questions 1 and 2 in the affirmative, it might be helpful to delve a little deeper by asking them, "What do you think you would have if your boss gave you the raise you were expecting?" The answer might be that they would feel more valued for their work. Instead of doing the inquiry on "My boss didn't give me a raise in my salary this year," we might do the inquiry on the statement "My boss doesn't value me."

By rephrasing the statement, we can identify the underlying need or desire driving the client's thoughts and feelings. In this case, there is a need for recognition. This can open the door to a much deeper inquiry, allowing your client to explore how they can meet their need for recognition in other ways.

We all know that catastrophizing is a cognitive bias and a type of negative thinking pattern where an individual excessively exaggerates the potential negative consequences of a situation. It is characterized by believing that a situation is far worse than it actually is and will have dire and permanent consequences.

The individual may also believe that they cannot cope with the situation and that it is out of their control. For example, suppose an individual experiences a significant loss, such as the loss of a job. In that case, they may catastrophize by believing that they will never find a job again, that they will be destitute forever, and that they will be unable to move on. So, by asking the individual to imagine the worst that could happen, we can generate their list of fears and take them to inquiry.

As a psychotherapist, it may be helpful to explore the underlying beliefs that contribute to feelings of anger. One approach could be to examine the use of "should" or "shouldn't" in statements related to the source of the anger. For example, instead of focusing on the statement "I am angry at my father because he hit me," which may elicit feelings of certainty and closure, reframing the statement to "My father shouldn't have hit me" may open up the possibility for deeper examination and understanding of the underlying beliefs and emotions that drive the anger. This approach may allow for a more nuanced exploration of the situation and may ultimately lead to greater insight and healing.

It may be important to encourage clients to critically examine their beliefs and perceptions to gain a deeper understanding of themselves and their experiences. One way to do this is to encourage clients to actively question and examine their "proofs" or evidence supporting their beliefs. This process of inquiry, which includes questioning their "evidence" using the four questions and turnaround method, can help clients evaluate their beliefs' validity and potentially uncover deeper truths. Additionally, it's important to remind clients that sometimes, even if something feels true, it doesn't necessarily mean it is true. It's important to be open to the possibility that their understanding of the situation may change through the process of inquiry.

As we transition to the next chapter, we will delve deeper into the critiques and challenges associated with The Work. By examining these perspectives, we can better equip ourselves to address and navigate any concerns that may arise in clinical practice, ensuring a balanced and informed approach. Join me as we explore these critiques and continue to refine our understanding and application of The Work.

## SUMMARY

- When stuck during an inquiry, use strategies to gain deeper insight.
- Use the phrase, "and it means that" to uncover underlying interpretations and assumptions.
- Identify the underlying needs or desires driving the client's thoughts and feelings.
- Encourage clients to imagine the worst that could happen to address catastrophizing.
- Examine the use of "should" or "shouldn't" in statements to explore underlying beliefs.
- Encourage clients to question their "proofs" or evidence supporting their beliefs.
- Remind clients that sometimes, even if something feels true, it doesn't necessarily mean it is true.

## REFLECTION QUESTIONS

1. When has asking a client "and that means that" unlocked a new perspective for you in therapy? What was the shift in understanding that occurred for the client?

2. Can you think of a time when you helped a client uncover the underlying beliefs or assumptions leading to their suffering? What was your process of inquiry like in that situation?

3. How might you apply the suggestions around catastrophic thinking to your work with clients who tend to catastrophize situations? What kinds of reframing or inquiry questions might be helpful?

4. In what ways have you encouraged clients to examine their "proofs" or evidence for their beliefs? What was the outcome when a client realized their perception may not fully reflect reality?

5. When has a process of inquiry led a client to a deeper understanding of themselves or their experiences? What made that particular inquiry effective or transformational?

# CHAPTER 16

## Critiques of The Work

It is essential to explore the critiques of The Work. To gain a deeper understanding of these critiques, I conducted an online survey of therapists using The Work to collect additional opinions and challenges of using The Work in clinical practice. Consequently, I have developed a list of criticisms to address their concerns. I hope to provide an overview of the critiques of The Work and to shed light on any misunderstandings. In Chapter 18, we will delve into the scientific inquiries and research studies centered around The Work.

### Re-traumatization of Patients with PTSD

Some critics have warned about the potential risks of re-traumatization and triggering when using The Work of Byron Katie in the treatment of PTSD. As seasoned psychotherapists, we're no strangers to the complexities of trauma and the intricacies of treating PTSD. So, it's entirely valid to be cautious when considering incorporating The Work of Byron Katie into your practice for such cases. The intensive self-inquiry that The Work demands can be a double-edged sword. While it can catalyze profound shifts in perspective, it can also lead to triggering and re-traumatization if not handled with extreme care.

Before diving into The Work with a trauma-affected client, it's non-negotiable to perform a thorough readiness assessment. This includes a formal clinical assessment using tools like the PCL-5 to evaluate PTSD symptom severity, as well as a self-report. A simple conversation about their feelings about self-inquiry and challenging core beliefs can provide invaluable insights. One approach is to initiate a trial period focusing on less emotionally charged topics. Observe how they respond, always staying vigilant for signs of distress or re-traumatization.

Preparation and safety planning are paramount. Establish emotional anchors your client can use for grounding—deep breathing exercises, tactile engagement, or a 'safe place' visualization. Ensure your client has a robust support system outside your sessions to help them process any emotional overflow. If your client displays signs of distress, have an exit strategy to de-escalate the situation.

So, who are the best candidates for incorporating The Work in treating PTSD? Generally, clients with high cognitive awareness and insight into their emotional states are more likely to benefit. Those who are highly motivated for change and have stable emotional support systems can also be more receptive to the challenges and rewards of this approach. However, there are certain cases where caution is advised. For instance, clients experiencing severe dissociation, unmanaged hyperarousal symptoms, or those who have a limited emotional vocabulary may not be suitable candidates for The Work.

When implemented carefully, the benefits can be transformative for your clients struggling with PTSD symptoms. Many clients experience a reduction in emotional suffering and a transition from a victim mindset to a more empowered, accountable perspective. Cognitive clarity often follows the challenging of destructive beliefs, allowing for a liberation that can be both surprising and profoundly relieving. Ultimately, The Work can foster emotional resilience and self-empowerment, providing a path to personal growth and greater psychological freedom.

## Lack of Empirical Evidence

Many have argued that The Work of Byron Katie, while popular and widely praised, suffers from a lack of empirical evidence to support its effectiveness. This lack of empirical evidence makes it difficult for mental health professionals to recommend or integrate The Work into their practice confidently.

While it is true that The Work of Byron Katie lacks extensive empirical evidence, there are emerging quantitative and qualitative studies and reports that suggest its potential benefits. I will discuss some of those studies in a later chapter. Many clients have reported experiencing positive shifts in their mental health and well-being after engaging in The Work. As research in this area continues to grow, it is essential to remain open to the possibility that The Work may offer a valuable therapeutic approach for some people. Additionally, The Work is not intended to replace professional mental health care but rather a complementary tool you and your clients can use alongside other treatments.

CBT is one of the most researched psychotherapeutic techniques. The parallels between CBT and The Work are evident. Both focus on challenging and changing cognitive distortions and behaviors. However, The Work goes deeper, adding a spiritual dimension that many find healing. It's a bridge between the mental and the transcendent.

## Oversimplification

The perception that The Work is overly simple or could be construed as victim-blaming is a concern I've heard, too. It's essential to realize that when misunderstood or misapplied, any therapeutic approach can create more harm than good. However, when understood deeply, The Work offers far more than simplistic solutions; it provides a nuanced way for clients, including those with histories of abuse, to challenge limiting beliefs and explore alternative perspectives.

First, let's clarify that turnarounds are not a form of victim-blaming. Quite the contrary. They are not directives or prescriptions but explorations. Clients are never asked to accept these turnarounds as ultimate truths; instead, they're like a fitting room for perspectives. I appreciate Byron Katie's metaphor: The turnarounds are like trying out different shoes in a shoe store; you only take home what fits you. This gives the clients the power of choice, making them active participants in their healing journey.

It's important to underscore that this empowerment is particularly crucial for clients who've been victims of abuse. Such clients have often been stripped of their agency, voice, and autonomy. They may feel trapped by their experiences, locked into a singular perspective that fosters a victim mentality. With turnarounds, these clients can explore other angles and dimensions of their thought patterns, some of which may be more empowering or freeing. While the trauma remains a fact, the interpretation of that trauma is complex and multi-faceted.

For instance, consider a client who holds the belief, "I am weak because I was abused." A potential turnaround might be, "I am strong because I was abused." The client doesn't have to accept this turnaround as a new belief; simply entertaining it opens up a space for recognizing resilience and strength. Even if they reject this turnaround, considering alternative perspectives can be empowering.

It's crucial to approach the turnarounds with sensitivity and timing, especially when working with abuse victims. They shouldn't be rushed into this phase of The Work; they must be emotionally ready to confront such challenging perspectives. And when they are, it's a clear sign of their readiness to shift from a state of victimhood toward one of empowerment.

The turnarounds provide a 360-degree view of the situation causing stress. Clients can choose which angle resonates with them and may help them move forward. When properly facilitated, this process can be far from an act of victim-blaming. Instead, it can be a decisive step toward reclaiming agency, challenging old narratives, and encouraging psychological growth and healing.

## Fear of Loss of Autonomy

Some of my colleagues have commented that The Work takes away personal autonomy because it encourages individuals to question and potentially discard deeply held beliefs and narratives. Since the process involves rigorously examining one's thoughts and beliefs, this could be perceived as a way of undermining or invalidating an individual's personal experiences or feelings. There's also a concern that individuals might become overly reliant on the process, using it as a crutch rather than trusting their judgment or intuition.

In my experience, The Work never tells the client what to think or do. Instead, The Work is a tool for self-inquiry that can help your clients gain clarity and make more empowered choices. By examining their beliefs and assumptions, clients can identify areas where they may be limiting themselves or holding themselves back. This can lead to greater self-awareness and a greater sense of personal agency.

It is also essential to understand the difference between acceptance and resignation. Acceptance is an active state that comes from understanding. In resignation, there is a passive state of "giving up." The Work never encourages inaction. However, it's important to understand that The Work is no magic bullet. Like meditation, for most people, the process of inquiry is a lifelong process.

Far from removing autonomy, The Work promotes self-awareness. By understanding the origin and impact of their beliefs, individuals can make more informed and conscious choices. This heightened self-awareness can increase personal autonomy as individuals are no longer blindly driven by unexamined beliefs.

### Insufficient Focus on Emotions

Some critics feel that The Work, in its quest for cognitive reframing, might sometimes overlook the human element. They describe it as lacking genuine empathy and compassion, essential components in any therapeutic approach. The Work emphasizes cognitive questioning and reframing of beliefs, which critics argue might overlook the importance of emotional processing and expression. For example, a client who struggles with unresolved grief might need to engage in deep emotional work to process their feelings, which The Work's focus on cognitive questioning might not address effectively.

The Work's focus on cognitive reframing doesn't negate the importance of empathy. Instead, it offers a different pathway to healing. For many, this direct approach feels refreshingly honest and devoid of patronization, allowing them to confront their issues head-on. The Work's cognitive questioning can be integrated with emotional processing and expression, providing clients with a holistic approach to addressing their thoughts, beliefs, and emotions. By challenging beliefs it often brings emotions to the forefront, allowing for deeper exploration and understanding. As you well know, the cognitive and emotional are intertwined, and The Work can serve as a bridge between the two. The Work can facilitate deep, transformative healing by encouraging your clients to explore their thoughts and feelings. I find using the Order of Creation Chart in Chapter 5 very helpful for facilitating emotional expression. Some of my less emotionally literate clients have found using the list of emotions in Chapter 5 also very helpful to name their emotions.

## Potential for Spiritual Bypassing

The potential for spiritual bypassing is an important concern to be aware of in any therapeutic approach with a spiritual component. The Work of Byron Katie is no exception. Spiritual bypassing can be a pitfall, especially when clients are newly introduced to the process. They may get caught up in the seemingly transcendent nature of the questions, skipping over the raw, emotional depths that require real work. Phrases like "Can you absolutely know that it's true?" can become almost like mantras that numb rather than enlighten if not used with the other three questions and turnarounds of The Work.

Your role as an experienced therapist is crucial here. The first step is to identify signs of spiritual bypassing in your clients. Watch for avoidance behaviors, like gravitating toward lofty spiritual concepts while neglecting to address emotional wounds. If you notice this pattern, it's an opportunity to intervene and redirect the focus back to genuine self-exploration.

Encourage your clients to honestly sit with their emotions and confront the underlying issues they might be avoiding. The Work is not about escaping pain but about understanding it, putting it into perspective, and transforming the relationship with it. For example, if a client deflects a conversation about their emotional pain by questioning its validity—"Can I absolutely know this is true?"—steer them back to the lived experience of that pain. Ask them to explore the origin of their emotions, the triggers, and how these emotional states manifest in their daily lives. This kind of focused attention can pave the way for meaningful emotional processing.

Don't just limit The Work to the cognitive domain; integrate it with somatic techniques to ground the experience in the body. Encourage clients to locate where in their body they feel the emotional tension when exploring a stressful thought. This creates a rich tapestry of cognitive and somatic awareness that can deepen the therapeutic process.

Also, it's vital to pace the therapy appropriately. Unveil the layers of emotional and spiritual complexity gradually, without overwhelming the client or trivializing their experience. This pacing safeguards against the 'quick-fix' mentality that often accompanies spiritual bypassing.

One powerful way to enhance emotional honesty is by creating a therapeutic environment where vulnerability is accepted and celebrated. When clients feel safe enough to expose their fears, pains, and inadequacies, the spiritual aspects of The Work can serve as a transformative rather than a bypassing force. In this context, the questions and the turnarounds of The Work become tools for profound self-inquiry, catalyzing emotional and spiritual growth.

Maintaining this balanced, grounded approach ensures that The Work is an instrument for authentic spiritual and emotional healing rather than an escape hatch. As therapists, we possess the skills and the ethical commitment to guide our clients through this nuanced journey, encouraging them to engage with both the emotional and the spiritual dimensions of their being.

The connection between the body and the mind is a foundational concept in psychotherapy. Cognitive shifts are vital, but so are the corresponding somatic shifts that anchor and amplify these mental changes. In this context, dismissing The Work as "somatic theatre" grossly undervalues its potential. It isn't mere performance; it's a practice deeply rooted in the psychosomatic fabric of human experience.

Let's consider the sequence of The Work, starting with the identification of a stressful thought. While this step is cognitive, the body is already involved, as stressful thoughts generally manifest as physical sensations or disturbances—tightness in the chest, a knot in the stomach, a tension headache, and so forth. When you guide clients through this process, invite them to connect with these sensations. Ask them how the thought feels in their body. This immediately makes the experience multidimensional, engaging both cognitive and somatic layers.

As the client moves through the four questions and the turnarounds, the body becomes an arena for testing new perspectives. For example, after a successful turnaround, you might notice a client's shoulders drop, their breath deepen, or their facial expression soften. These are not mere theatrics but visceral confirmations of a cognitive shift. Encourage your clients to note these bodily changes. Ask them, "How does your body feel when you consider this new perspective?" These reflections anchor the new understanding of bodily experience, making it more tangible and real. My friend and fellow psychotherapist in the Bay Area, Ken Farber, agrees. According to him, the clients who report this "somatic shift" are the ones who stick with the practice of The Work.

Incorporating somatic markers also provides another layer of validation or challenge for the turnarounds. If a client says they're okay with a new perspective, but their body language screams discomfort, that incongruence becomes a point of exploration. "Your words say one thing, but your body seems to say another. What's going on here?" This query can often lead to deeper layers of understanding and resistance that might not emerge through cognitive inquiry alone.

Moreover, integrating somatic awareness into The Work complements other body-oriented therapeutic approaches you may already use, such as Somatic Experiencing or Sensorimotor Psychotherapy. You can weave these modalities together, offering your clients a rich, embodied path to healing. For instance, you can use grounding techniques to help clients center themselves before diving into the challenging aspects of The Work or employ somatic markers to gauge the resonance of a turnaround.

## Lack of Formal Training

Byron Katie's lack of formal training in psychology has been a point of criticism, with detractors arguing that her approach may be insufficient for treating mental illness. While formal training and credentials offer a structured understanding of mental health issues, they are not the sole determinants of efficacy in therapeutic interventions.

Let's start by acknowledging the roots of many therapeutic techniques, which often begin as deeply personal experiences or intuitive understandings before undergoing formal academic validation. The Work is no exception. Born from Byron Katie's personal journey, it resonates deeply with many because it emerged from the crucible of human suffering and self-inquiry. This "authenticity factor" can often reach people in ways that more sterile, academically-conceived methods cannot.

Katie has never advocated for The Work as a stand-alone treatment for severe mental illnesses. The clinicians I know often applied The Work within the context of their broader therapeutic approach, integrated by bringing their formal training into the mix. As experienced therapists, you have the ability to adapt The Work, combining it with other evidence-based treatments for a more comprehensive strategy tailored to each individual's needs.

Critics point to the risk of misinterpreting the needs of clients with specific mental health challenges. This is where your expertise comes in. With your foundational knowledge in psychology, you can identify the limitations and potentials of The Work in treating various mental health issues. You can also better assess whether a client is suited for this type of intervention or whether a different approach would be more effective.

Moreover, psychotherapy is rife with examples of practices that have gained empirical support over time despite their unconventional origins. Mindfulness, for instance, is a Buddhist practice and has only recently been rigorously studied and integrated into mainstream psychology. The Buddha had no academic qualifications. The Work could well follow a similar trajectory as more clinicians like you incorporate it into their practices and study its effects.

### The Work is a Cult

In addressing concerns about The Work of Byron Katie being a cult, it is crucial to emphasize that The Work fundamentally opposes the central concept of a cult. While cults typically require indoctrination and unquestioning acceptance of prescribed beliefs, The Work empowers individuals to question and analyze their own beliefs, advocating for a personal journey towards self-awareness and critical thinking. This process involves reclaiming one's mental autonomy rather than simply replacing old beliefs with new dogmas. The core of The Work is about shedding the layers of conditioned, fear-based thinking that constrain our lives.

Byron Katie herself emphasizes this point in her book, "Loving What Is," stating, "What I love about The Work is that it allows you to go inside and find your own happiness, to experience what already exists within you, unchanging, immovable, ever-present, ever-waiting. You are the teacher you've been waiting for. You are the one who can end your own suffering." Her approach encourages introspection and self-guidance, urging each person to explore what is true for themselves, rather than being dictated by her or any doctrine.

When considering whether The Work is a religion, it is more accurately described as a form of radical skepticism. It shares philosophical underpinnings with Zen koans and Socratic dialogue—tools designed to provoke deep personal insight rather than adhering to any specific religious or cultural tradition. Originating from the practical insights of an ordinary individual, The Work is both approachable and grounded in everyday experience.

Many criticisms of Byron Katie's Work reflect a lack of direct knowledge of the technique. For example, one critic watched a YouTube video of Katie facilitating a woman on stage and accused her of dominating the client, "reframing" the client's fear, and of "somatic theatre."

By "somatic theatre," the critic is highlighting the combination of Katie's body language, physical setting, and power dynamics that, in his view, contribute to a form of control that is more about performance and less about genuine therapeutic intervention. However, Katie's body language, such as leaning forward and making direct eye contact, can be interpreted as a form of active engagement and presence, essential qualities in any therapeutic relationship. Such gestures aim to create a connection, showing the participants that they are seen, heard, and understood.

Let's address the accusation that Byron Katie's technique is based on "dominance." The facilitator's role is not to impose but to guide. What might appear as leading the conversation is often a systematic attempt to help the client dissect deeply ingrained and often unexamined beliefs. This is a process rooted in empathy and the desire to assist the client in liberating themselves from their mental traps. The essence here is empowerment, not subjugation.

Now, let's talk about the tool of reframing, which has raised some eyebrows. Critics label it as manipulation, yet reframing is a standard tool in many therapeutic modalities. It's not about changing the story but offering a new lens through which to view it. This is especially vital for clients stuck in thought patterns that have tormented them for years if not decades. In reframing, a fresh narrative possibility is introduced, and clients can choose to adopt it or not; the agency remains with them.

Regarding the public setting where Katie often conducts The Work, it's worth noting that group dynamics have long been harnessed in therapeutic settings. From Alcoholics Anonymous to group therapies in various psychological disciplines, the shared experience often amplifies the healing process. Participants realize they are not alone in their struggles, creating a sense of community and collective empowerment.

The centrality of the client-agency differentiates The Work from a cultic environment. Your clients are taught to survive their mental tribulations and engage with them actively. They are empowered to question, challenge, and shift their perspectives, taking command of their emotional lives. This is antithetical to the very essence of cultic control and domination.

As therapists, understanding these nuances can help us better integrate The Work into our practice, harnessing its strengths while being mindful of its limitations.

## The Transformative Power of The Work: A New Paradigm

When taken out of context or applied without proper understanding, any therapeutic tool or technique can lead to misinterpretations. The essence of The Work is self-inquiry, which is a universal concept found in many therapeutic modalities. With proper guidance and genuine commitment to understanding its principles, The Work can be a transformative tool.

As you'll discover by exploring The Work and how you can use it in your clinical practice with powerful and transformative results, a new paradigm in psychotherapy is emerging that focuses on the awareness behind thoughts rather than the content of thoughts themselves. This shift in focus is already starting to yield positive results as you and your client alike begin to explore the space between thoughts. In this space, there is a quieter awareness that is not completely dominated by the thinker. From this more peaceful place, seeing thoughts for what they are becomes possible: transient mental constructs that do not necessarily reflect reality. This understanding can lead to a more profound sense of peace and well-being.

Alongside this shift, another groundbreaking development in the field of psychotherapy is the resurgence of interest in psychedelic-assisted therapy. Psychedelics, such as psilocybin, LSD, and MDMA, are being studied for their potential to catalyze profound insights and facilitate lasting psychological healing when used in a controlled therapeutic setting. This approach represents a new paradigm that recognizes the value of non-ordinary states of consciousness in the healing process. By allowing individuals to access expanded states of awareness, psychedelic-assisted therapy can help them gain fresh perspectives on their thoughts, emotions, and past experiences, leading to significant breakthroughs and personal growth.

As the field of psychotherapy evolves, it is likely that these new paradigms will continue to gain popularity as they provide more effective ways of helping people heal from their past and live in the reality of this moment.

## SUMMARY

- The Work lacks empirical evidence: Emerging studies suggest its potential benefits. It is complementary to professional mental health care. Parallels with CBT exist, with The Work adding a spiritual dimension.
- The Work might overlook the human element, potentially lacking empathy and compassion: The Work's focus on cognitive reframing offers an honest pathway to healing that can integrate with emotional processing.
- The technique is based on "dominance" and lacks genuine therapeutic intervention: The facilitator's role is to guide, rooted in empathy, aiming for client empowerment.
- The tool of reframing in The Work is seen as manipulation: Reframing is a standard tool in therapy. It offers a new perspective, and the agency remains with the client.
- Public settings for The Work might not be beneficial: Group dynamics have long been used in therapeutic settings, amplifying the healing process and fostering a sense of community.
- The Work offers a new paradigm in psychotherapy focusing on the awareness behind thoughts.

## REFLECTION QUESTIONS

1. As you read about the various critiques of The Work, which one resonated with you the most? Why do you think that particular critique stood out?

2. How might you address some of the concerns or misunderstandings people have expressed about The Work with your clients?

3. What role do you see spirituality playing in your clinical practice? How might you integrate spiritual aspects of The Work while still ensuring emotional processing for clients?

4. Do any of The Work's critiques make you hesitate about incorporating it into your practice? Why or why not?

5. How do you currently help clients become aware of the space between thoughts? What excites or concerns you about this new paradigm of focusing on awareness rather than thought content?

# CHAPTER 17

## The Challenges and Rewards of Doing The Work in Clinical Settings

Have you ever reached an impasse in therapy where even time-tested interventions fall short? What are the specific challenges you might encounter in a clinical setting? And how can you navigate them to truly deepen your practice? In this chapter, we explore insights from therapists who have incorporated The Work into their practices.

This chapter will discuss my experiences and the experiences of other clinicians who have implemented The Work in their clinical practice. These stories give you insights into how you can benefit from this powerful technique.

My insights into applying The Work of Byron Katie in clinical contexts stem from multiple sources. As a psychotherapist and facilitator of The Work, my direct experiences have been the most significant influence shaping my reflections on this topic.

As a therapist and facilitator of The Work, I've gained valuable insights into how this powerful method can be integrated into clinical practice. My own experiences, along with feedback from a survey of over 100 mental health professionals who have completed the School for The Work training, have shed light on the many benefits and diverse applications of this approach.

Therapists who use The Work in their practice consistently report that it is a simple yet highly effective tool for helping clients understand their thoughts and beliefs and how these affect their overall well-being. They appreciate how the method empowers clients to take responsibility for their beliefs and manage their own suffering while providing a gentle, non-pathologizing space for self-exploration.

One of the standout features of The Work is its versatility. Practitioners can use it as a standalone approach or seamlessly integrate it with other modalities such as CBT, mindfulness, EFT, hypnosis, and NLP. This flexibility allows therapists to create tailored treatment plans that address clients' unique needs and preferences.

The Work has proven to be a valuable tool in a wide range of settings, from individual and group therapy sessions to anger management classes, DBT groups, and even elementary schools. Many therapists have also found success incorporating The Work into substance abuse treatment programs that utilize a 12-step approach and cognitive behavioral therapy.

While the survey results overwhelmingly support the effectiveness of The Work in clinical practice, it's important to acknowledge that there may be situations where this method is not the most appropriate choice. Later in this chapter, we'll explore some of these instances in more detail.

Here are some of their responses when asked: "What do you think are the main advantages of The Work compared to other counseling approaches you have trained in?"

- It is much faster and deals with the present rather than dwelling on the past.
- It cuts through issues and helps people move past their stories.

- It is not associated with religion, which may appeal to those who are skeptical or suspicious of traditional therapy or religion.
- It helps people see truth and reality quickly.
- It allows for the immediate release of stress and healing.
- It is simple yet profound.
- It is non-judgmental and provides a sense of safety, which allows for opening up.
- It provides a real opportunity for transformation.
- It can be taught and taken with the person for life, allowing them to go directly in the important direction inward.
- It empowers your client and reduces dependency on the therapist or institution.
- It can be used in any setting and remove all the stories other therapies tend to foster.
- It leads your client into non-dual awareness.
- It is simple and straightforward.
- Your client uses their own words that are powerful and non-shaming.
- It is quick and effective.

When asked, "What are the main disadvantages of The Work in clinical settings?" Here's what the respondents said:

- It is not widely accepted and not sanctioned by mainstream mental health organizations.
- It can appear invalidating or harsh to some people.
- It is not appropriate for all clients and requires a certain level of mental and emotional stability.
- Some clients may find it challenging to concentrate and use their imagination.

- There is difficulty getting trained or finding qualified practitioners.
- It can be difficult for clients to accept their role in their problems.
- It requires a high degree of skill and experience from the practitioner.
- Some practitioners may use it exclusively when other interventions would be more appropriate.
- There is a lack of long-term studies on its effectiveness.
- Some clients may find it confusing to balance the concepts of passiveness and activeness.
- Some may find it challenging to solve specific fears and anxieties through The Work.
- Some clients may feel unheard or not heard, and the relationship and trust between client and clinician may differ from traditional talk therapy.
- The Work requires compassion, self-reflection, and personal strength, which not all counselors may possess.
- Lastly, they also reported that it is more effective when the therapist has also done a lot of Work themselves.

Now, let us look at how clients who come to a psychotherapy setting differ from those seeking The Work from facilitators.

Individuals who come to the facilitation of The Work are often highly motivated and willing to take ownership of their thoughts and actions. They might already be familiar with The Work and a goal or issue they would like to address using self-inquiry and questioning. On the other hand, clients visiting psychotherapists may have less enthusiasm for altering their life situation. They may be working through more complex issues, such as unresolved traumas, long-term habits, or deep-rooted emotions. In this environment, a more gradual and supportive approach is typically adopted to help them explore their difficulties and commit to changes in their lives.

The Work can be successfully used in a variety of clinical situations, such as with individuals and groups of relatively healthy adults in transition and crisis, semi-intellectual types, couples therapy, clients who are in later stages of recovery from sexual abuse and physical trauma, grief counseling, low levels of emotional dysregulation, addiction recovery, relationship issues, depression, anxiety, family or friend resentments, etc. Motivated individuals who are tired enough of living with the kind of suffering they have had for most of their lives and who are ready to accept the reality that they alone can change tend to do well.

Even though The Work is a potent form of self-examination that can benefit many kinds of problems and issues, it may not be suitable or feasible to do it under certain circumstances. Some clients may find it too simple or intellectual, and others may need help to go deep enough to experience real change. Here are some situations where The Work may not be the best option. None of these situations and disorders listed below are absolute contraindications for using The Work:

- The Work is not recommended for use with clinically unstable clients, such as those with severe dissociative identity disorder, paranoid schizophrenia, or other forms of active psychosis. Someone going through an acute manic phase of bipolar disorder may not be able to focus enough to answer the questions. Their impaired reasoning abilities and difficulty with self-inquiry could make it unsuitable or impossible to do The Work.
- If a client is going through an extreme state of distress like severe depression, a tendency to self-harm, or having acute suicidal thoughts, doing The Work may not be the right approach until their mental health has improved. It is first necessary to address their safety and provide appropriate support.

- It is also advisable to tread carefully while doing the turnarounds with those in the early stages of recovery from abuse—either physical or sexual trauma. Clients who have gone through severe trauma or abuse may not feel safe enough to engage in self-inquiry without addressing the underlying impact of the trauma first.
- Similarly, it may be inappropriate for clients with cognitive impairments, such as intellectual disabilities, dementia, or difficulty with abstract thought. Their ability to understand and engage in self-inquiry may be limited.
- For those with severe personality disorders, such as narcissistic personality disorder, borderline personality disorder, or antisocial personality disorder, it is best to hold off using The Work until trust, rapport, and an excellent therapeutic alliance are established.
- The Work may not be practical for clients in the early stages of detoxification. It is best to wait till they are medically and emotionally more stable before introducing The Work.
- Those with severe attachment/detachment disorder or highly traumatized or reactive in sessions are often not good candidates for The Work.
- It may also be less beneficial for court-ordered clients or those not motivated to answer the questions truthfully.
- Clients with deep religious beliefs or rigid points of view often do not do well with The Work.
- As a general rule, the effectiveness of The Work also depends on the client's level of openness and ability to self-reflect.
- Lastly, I would only use The Work with clients who are open to it or motivated to engage in the inquiry process. And then there are some clients who like The Work but are either unable or unwilling to go deep enough in order for them to experience real change.

It is important to note that The Work should not be considered a replacement for professional help, and seeking appropriate medical care should always be prioritized when dealing with complex mental health issues. When deciding whether to use The Work for any given situation, it is essential to consider each individual's needs and circumstances. It's vital to assess the readiness and willingness of your client before proceeding with The Work so they can benefit from it.

It's important to note that The Work process is about more than just answering the four questions. It's also about listening to the answers and the feelings that come up during the process. Suppose a client is just intellectually answering the questions without exploring the emotions and experiences that come up. In that case, they may not fully engage in the process and may be unable to gain the full benefits. Done right, this deep process can lead to personal growth, a shift in perspective, decreased emotional suffering, and increased peace and well-being.

For almost a year after I came across The Work, I admit that I was doing it intellectually, most of the time doing it in my head and going straight to the turnarounds. As I mentioned, most of my professional work was done on a large university campus, so many of my clients were highly intellectual. Howard was one such man. Howard was 35 and seeking help for anxiety and relationship struggles. He was highly analytical and tended to approach challenges logically. When I first introduced him to The Work of Byron Katie, Howard responded to the four questions intellectually without fully diving into the process. For example, when I asked him, "Is it true that your partner never listens to you?" he responded, "Yes, but that's just my perception, and it's not necessarily accurate."

As his therapist, I saw the need to help Howard break through this intellectual block. I started by encouraging him to connect with his emotions and to understand the connection between his thoughts, feelings, and behaviors using the Think→Feel→Behave→Result cycle we discussed earlier. I challenged Howard to question his limiting thoughts and beliefs and to consider the evidence for and against them.

Therapist: "Can you describe your feelings and mental images when you think about your partner not listening to you?"

Howard: "I feel like I'm not important when my partner never listens to me."

Therapist: "So when your partner doesn't listen to you, you conclude that you are not important. Can you trace the origin of this belief? How long have you held onto it?"

Howard: "I've had it for a while. It stems from past experiences with partners not listening."

Throughout the process, I worked to cultivate a supportive and trusting relationship with Howard. As therapy sessions progressed, I helped him discover alternative perspectives to his thoughts. I encouraged him to explore different points of view and to challenge his assumptions about himself and his partner. I created a safe space for him to be open and honest and reminded him that The Work is a journey that takes time and persistence to see results.

As Howard continued to engage in The Work, he gained a deeper understanding of how his thoughts and beliefs affected his relationships. This deeper understanding led him to practice The Work more diligently. Within a few months, he noticed a significant decrease in his anxiety levels and an improvement in his relationships.

I want to share with you some of my reasons why people who tend to be intellectual may have difficulty doing The Work.

- **Fear of change:** Some people may resist change and be unwilling to engage in the self-inquiry process fully. They may be more comfortable intellectually answering the questions rather than exploring their thoughts and feelings.
- **Fear of emotions:** Some people may be uncomfortable with their feelings and unwilling to explore them fully. They may find it easier to answer questions intellectually and avoid exploring their feelings.
- **Lack of understanding:** Some people may need to understand The Work's purpose and process fully and learn how to engage in the process thoroughly. They may answer the questions intellectually because they don't know how to do it otherwise.
- **Lack of motivation:** Some people may need more reason to engage in The Work fully. They may be answering the questions intellectually because they need to see the value in doing the process correctly.

It's important to note that everyone is different and may have various reasons for answering the questions intellectually. Additionally, it's essential to understand that if someone is not fully engaged in the process, the outcome may be less effective than when fully engaged.

What are some of the things that can be done to help and guide individuals to go deeper?

Some effective strategies include:

- **Providing guidance and support:** Offering guidance and support helps clients understand the process of The Work and how to engage in it fully. This also includes providing a safe and non-judgmental environment for clients to explore their thoughts and feelings.
- **Encouraging honesty and self-exploration:** It is crucial for clients to be honest with themselves and explore their thoughts and feelings fully. It's important to remind them that the process is not about being right or wrong but about understanding their perspective and how it affects them.
- **Asking questions and providing prompts:** Asking questions and providing prompts can help clients go deeper and fully explore their thoughts and feelings. This also allows them to identify any resistance to questioning their thoughts and beliefs.
- **Providing feedback:** Offering feedback helps clients understand how they engage in the process and where they may be able to go deeper. This also involves identifying patterns or themes in their thoughts and beliefs.

Additionally, helping clients understand the connection between their thoughts and emotions and how their thoughts can affect them, using the Thinking→Feeling→Behavior→Outcome diagram discussed in Chapter 2, can be beneficial.

Creating a safe and supportive environment: It is essential to establish a safe and supportive environment where clients can feel comfortable exploring their thoughts and feelings. Encouraging clients to take their time and go at their own pace is critical to creating this environment.

Overall, our goal as clinicians is to help our clients fully engage in the process of The Work and provide guidance and support to help them go deeper and understand their thoughts and beliefs.

In my experience, while it is uncommon, some clients may misuse The Work and the turnarounds as a form of self-punishment. This often stems from deep-seated feelings of guilt, shame, or inadequacy. They may believe that punishing themselves can atone for past mistakes or perceived shortcomings.

One way this manifests is by fixating solely on negative thoughts and beliefs, such as "I'm not good enough" or "I'm a failure." Instead of questioning and examining these thoughts through The Work, they use the turnarounds to berate themselves further.

When you observe this pattern, guiding your clients towards self-compassion and kindness is crucial. Remind them that everyone makes mistakes and that the key is to learn from them and move forward. Help them identify and challenge the self-critical thoughts fueling their self-punishment.

Emphasize that for most people, The Work is a gradual process, not a quick fix. Encourage patience and persistence as they work through their thoughts and beliefs. Consistency and self-compassion are essential for proper growth and healing.

Practicing The Work has dramatically enhanced my skills as a therapist. By examining and challenging my stressful thoughts about demanding clients, I've been able to facilitate more successful and rewarding treatment outcomes. The Work helps me stay fully present with my clients, fostering deeper attunement and stronger therapeutic alliances.

## SUMMARY

- The Work is an uncomplicated yet potent therapy technique that blends seamlessly with other therapies.
- It stresses the significance of the present moment, providing clients with the power to take charge of their thoughts and actions.
- However, practitioners must evaluate a client's readiness and skill level before employing it. The Work may not be appropriate for individuals dealing with severe mental health issues or those in early recovery from trauma.
- Practicing The Work can enhance therapeutic abilities and foster stronger relationships. Nonetheless, it should be noted that The Work cannot replace professional assistance.

# REFLECTION QUESTIONS

1. As a psychotherapist, what opportunities and challenges do you see in incorporating The Work into your practice? How might you address any challenges that arise?

2. What kind of clients do you think would benefit most from The Work? Are there any clients you would hesitate to use this technique with?

3. What resonated with you most in reading about the experiences of other therapists using The Work clinically? Were there any surprises or insights?

4. How might your self-inquiry and personal experience with The Work affect your ability to facilitate it for clients? What internal work might you need to do first?

5. What support systems (supervision, consultation, training, etc.) might help you feel prepared to effectively bring The Work into your practice?

6. As you read about the advantages and disadvantages of using The Work clinically, what key takeaways did you gain? How might you mitigate any potential disadvantages in your practice?

7. In what ways do you feel called to take action after reading this chapter? What first steps will you take to incorporate The Work with your clients?

# CHAPTER 18

## Research and Future Directions

In this concluding chapter, I'd like to take you through the published literature on the effectiveness of using The Work of Byron Katie in therapy. Surprisingly, there have only been a few randomized controlled clinical trials of her work. Though it is challenging to measure the clinical efficacy of The Work, there are several good quality studies published in peer-reviewed journals as well as Ph.D. and Master's level qualitative research studies that can provide some insight into its potential benefits. Generally speaking, authors have found that The Work is associated with increased self-awareness, improved ability to manage difficult emotions, and an increased capacity to recognize and challenge negative thoughts resulting in increased well-being and quality of life. The Work is often termed "Inquiry-Based Stress Reduction or IBSR" in the clinical world.

To better understand what The Work looks like in action, I want to let you in on the syllabus for an 8-week program I used at the university, which has seen great success in achieving its goals. This program includes an introduction to The Work principles and methodology, guided inquiry exercises, homework assignments, and role-playing activities designed to help participants experience the benefits of The Work in their everyday lives.

Preliminary findings from an ongoing longitudinal study at Stanford University further support the potential of The Work in addressing mental health issues. In a personal communication, Dr. Ariel Ganz from the research team shared that over 90% of participants recovered from depression after engaging in The Work, with 95% sustaining recovery for at least 14 months (A. Ganz, personal communication, May 11, 2024). This study also explored various biological markers, finding changes that correlated with depression levels throughout the study.

Researchers at Stanford University and Tel-Aviv University conducted a randomized controlled trial to assess the impact of a 12-week Inquiry Based Stress Reduction (IBSR) intervention on various measures in adults who stutter. (Feldman, 2021) Fifty-six participants were randomly assigned to either the IBSR intervention group or a control group. The IBSR program involved weekly group sessions teaching participants to identify and question stressful thoughts.

Compared to the control group, the IBSR group showed significant improvements in their overall experience of stuttering, as measured by the Overall Assessment of the Speaker's Experience of Stuttering (OASES). This included better scores in general knowledge about stuttering, reactions to stuttering, communication in daily situations, and quality of life. The IBSR group also had significantly lower trait anxiety and higher satisfaction with life after the intervention. These benefits were maintained one month later.

Landau et al. conducted a randomized controlled trial to investigate the effects of a 12-week Inquiry-Based Stress Reduction (IBSR) intervention on psychological well-being, sleep quality, psychosocial variables, and attitudes towards risk-reducing surgery in women with BRCA variants in Israel. (Landau, 2021)

The study included 100 women, with 50 assigned to the IBSR group and 50 to the control group receiving standard care. Compared to the control group, the IBSR group showed significant improvements in all dimensions of psychological well-being, sleep quality, and a more favorable attitude towards risk-reducing surgical procedures, both immediately after the intervention and at a 12-week follow-up. The authors suggest that IBSR can be used as a self-practice tool to enhance well-being and support decision-making processes in women with BRCA variants.

In a prospective pilot clinical trial at the Tel-Aviv Medical Center in Israel, researchers evaluated the feasibility and effectiveness of Inquiry-Based Stress Reduction (IBSR) for improving the psychological and physical well-being of breast cancer survivors. (Lev-Ari et al, 2013). Twenty-nine participants attended 12 weekly group sessions, each lasting 3.5 hours, and engaged in individual practice for at least 60 minutes per week. Of these, 24 women (82.75%) completed the program without any adverse effects, indicating the intervention's suitability for this population. Significant improvements were observed in sleep quality, fatigue levels, and various aspects of well-being, including physical, social, familial, emotional, and functional domains, as measured by the Functional Assessment of Cancer Therapy-Breast scale (FACT-B). These promising results suggest that IBSR could be a beneficial intervention for breast cancer survivors in a hospital setting.

In a separate study, Schnaider-Levi et al. investigated the impact of IBSR on teacher burnout using a quasi-experimental design. ((Schnaider-Levi et al., 2020)). Fifty-three teachers participated in a 12-week IBSR program, with the intervention group engaging for 4.5 hours weekly, while a passive control group was also included.

Compared to the control group, teachers in the intervention group experienced significant improvements in emotional exhaustion and personal accomplishment. This study highlights the potential of IBSR to enhance well-being and reduce burnout among teachers and other professionals in high-stress environments.

Eric Smernoff and colleagues investigated the effects of The Work on psychological symptoms and quality of life in a non-clinical sample. (Smernoff, 2015) Participants (n = 197) completed a nine-day training course and were assessed before, after, and six months post-intervention. The outcome measures included several well-established psychological assessment tools, such as the Beck Depression Inventory-II (BDI-II), Subjective Happiness Scale (SHS), Quality of Life Inventory (QOLI), Quick Inventory of Depressive Symptomatology-Self Report (QIDS-SR16), Outcome Questionnaire 45.2 (OQ-45.2), State-Trait Anger Expression Inventory-2 (STAXI-2), and State-Trait Anxiety Inventory (STAI).

The results, analyzed using a mixed models approach, revealed significant positive changes between baseline, the end of the intervention, and the six-month follow-up for all measured outcomes. Participants showed improvements in depression (BDI-II and QIDS-SR16), happiness (SHS), quality of life (QOLI), overall psychological distress (OQ-45.2), anger (STAXI-2 State and Trait), and anxiety (STAI State and Trait) scores. These findings suggest that The Work may be effective in improving psychological well-being and quality of life in the general population.

Tajnia, an ICU nurse and researcher conducted a quasi-experimental study aimed to investigate the effect of Inquiry-Based Stress Reduction (IBSR) on mortality awareness and interpersonal problems among intensive care unit (ICU) nurses in southeastern

Iran. (Tajnia, 2022) The study, conducted in 2021, utilized a pre-test-posttest design with a convenience sampling method. Nurses were divided into intervention (n=32) and control (n=35) groups using block randomization. The intervention group received two-hour IBSR counseling sessions weekly for six weeks.

Data were collected using the Multidimensional Mortality Awareness Measure and Inventory of Interpersonal Problems before, immediately after, and six weeks after the intervention. The results showed a significant increase in mortality awareness mean scores in the intervention group compared to the control group ($p<0.001$). Furthermore, the intervention group demonstrated lower interpersonal problems mean scores immediately after and six weeks after the intervention compared to before the intervention ($p<0.001$). In contrast, the control group experienced an increase in interpersonal problems over time ($p<0.001$).

The study concludes that IBSR is an appropriate intervention method to improve mortality awareness and reduce interpersonal problems among ICU nurses. These findings suggest that IBSR can be a valuable tool in helping ICU nurses cope with the stress and emotional challenges associated with caring for dying patients.

A pilot study investigated the potential of an intervention using Inquiry-Based Stress Reduction to address self-stigma among people living with HIV (PLHIV) in Zimbabwe (Ferris France N, 2019). 23 PLHIV took part in a 12-week IBSR program, with qualitative and quantitative data collected at baseline, post-intervention, and 3-month follow-up.

Results showed significant reductions in self-stigma, depression, and fears around disclosure, as well as improvements in daily activities, view of the future, and feelings around being HIV-positive. Qualitative findings revealed positive changes in participants' lives, including improved self-perception, relationships, and outlook on living with HIV.

Nadine and her colleagues concluded that the IBSR technique showed promise as a tool to help PLHIV overcome self-stigma and improve wellbeing.

Ms. Ferris France also published a qualitative study aimed to identify and gain understanding of the core beliefs underlying self-stigma among people living with HIV (PLHIV) in Ireland. (Ferris France, 2015) Semi-structured interviews and written statements were collected from 17 participants.

The analysis revealed four categories of core beliefs: disclosure, sexuality and sexual pleasure, self-perception, and body, illness and death. Participants reported beliefs such as being unclean, undeserving of sympathy, or unemployable due to their HIV status. The study also explored the functions of self-stigma, including maintaining a victim status, providing protection against stigma from others, and justifying non-disclosure.

Coping strategies used by participants were community involvement, personal development, and connection with others. The findings were incorporated into a conceptual framework of self-stigma. Understanding these core beliefs can inform the development of targeted interventions to help PLHIV overcome self-stigma and its negative impact on treatment adherence, access to services, and overall well-being.

Another prospective controlled trial investigated the effects of an Inquiry-Based Stress Reduction (IBSR) intervention on well-being, resilience, burnout, mindfulness, and stress among teachers in Israel during the COVID-19 pandemic. (Zadok-Gurman, 2021) The intervention group (n=35) participated in a 12-week IBSR program using blended learning (face-to-face and online), while the control group (n=32) did not receive the intervention.

The IBSR group showed significant improvements in psychological well-being, life satisfaction, positive affect, resilience, and mindfulness compared to the control group. Both groups experienced increased emotional exhaustion, but the increase was significantly lower in the IBSR group. No significant differences were found in perceived stress or personal accomplishment.

The authors conclude that the IBSR intervention enhanced resilience and improved subjective and psychological well-being among teachers, despite the challenges posed by the COVID-19 pandemic and lockdown in Israel. In contrast, the control group experienced decreased well-being and increased burnout.

Jacqui Luff, a mental health counselor and graduate of the University of Notre Dame in Australia, conducted a qualitative study exploring the Inquiry-Based Stress Reduction (IBSR) approach in counseling. (Luff, 2017) Her Master's thesis was designed to examine the experience of therapists using IBSR personally and in sessions with clients, uncover its challenges and limitations, identify its strengths and role as an intervention modality, and consider its affect on self-care and burnout prevention.

Six mental health professionals with IBSR certification were interviewed using a semi-structured format to gain an understanding of these topics. The gathered data were further analyzed using Interpretative Phenomenological Analysis (IPA). During the process, several key themes emerged, including the impact of IBSR on the therapist, the potential for self-care and burnout prevention, therapeutic benefits for clients and practitioners, challenges or limitations of the approach, and its potential to foster relationships between those involved. The findings indicate that IBSR has significant effects, with many practitioners reporting numerous benefits, including enhanced self-awareness. It also appeared that this approach could foster trust within the therapeutic alliance. However, certain shortcomings, such as difficulties encountered when working with clients who do not want to leave their story behind or misinterpreting concepts leading to blame, should not be forgotten either.

As a conclusion to her work, Luff emphasized that additional research into IBSR was needed while also ensuring that what was already known was considered when looking at methods for preventing burnout among helping professionals.

Meanwhile, in 2015, a Dutch psychotherapist, Marie Odiel van Rhijn, published a paper in the *European Society of Medicine.* She reviewed the results from several studies showing that IBSR effectively reduced stress, negative affect, and psychopathologic symptoms. She wrote about how IBSR had also been found to improve sleep quality, levels of fatigue, and various aspects of mental health such as self-esteem, satisfaction with life, sense of coherence, and positive and negative affect. However, she concluded that there are some limitations and pitfalls associated with the IBSR technique, such as the need for clients to be willing to examine their thoughts and the potential for clients to feel overwhelmed by the turnarounds. Despite these limitations, the findings suggest that IBSR could promote mental health and enhance psychological well-being.

The promising findings shared by Dr. Ariel Ganz above highlight the potential for The Work to create lasting positive changes in mental health and well-being. The observed biological changes associated with depression recovery further underscore the need for continued research into the mechanisms and long-term effects of this powerful tool.

As we come to the end of our shared journey, I hope that you feel ready to incorporate The Work into your work with clients. Learning any new skill requires practice and persistence, and you may encounter challenges along the way. However, by approaching these challenges with an open heart and mind, you can unlock new opportunities and help your clients develop greater self-awareness, which will improve their lives. Although we don't know where this journey will take us, remember that you are not alone on this path. I encourage you to explore the resources in the bibliography to develop your skills further using The Work.

## SUMMARY

- The Work can increase self-awareness, regulate emotions, and challenge negative thoughts.
- Qualitative research suggests potential benefits and inquiry-based stress reduction positively impacts therapists' and clients' self-care.
- The Work can alleviate stress, transform perceptions and behaviors, and improve psychological well-being and sleep quality.
- Incorporating The Work into therapy has promising potential for enhancing positive outcomes for clients.
- Consider trying The Work to inspire lasting change in your client's lives.

# REFLECTION QUESTIONS

1. In what ways do you think incorporating IBSR/The Work into your practice could benefit your clients? What outcomes might improve?

2. What limitations or challenges do you anticipate in integrating IBSR/The Work into your therapeutic approach? How could you address those?

3. How might utilizing IBSR/The Work affect your experience as a therapist? Could it help with burnout prevention or self-care?

4. Do any clients or issues that might be particularly suited to trying IBSR/The Work as an additional tool come to mind? Why?

5. Based on the research summarized, what excites you most about the potential for IBSR/The Work? What would you be most curious to see further research on?

# CONCLUSION

## The Journey Ahead

As you reach the final pages of this book, I hope you feel inspired to take the first steps on an exciting new journey. This journey involves bringing the transformative power of The Work of Byron Katie into your therapeutic practice.

In these pages, you've seen glimpses into the immense potential of The Work as a tool for emotional healing and personal transformation.

One of the most empowering gifts you can offer your clients is handing them the tools to take charge of their healing journeys. The Work provides a roadmap, offering clients a structured approach to building resilience, strength, and personal agency from within. Questioning their core narratives, you help liberate their inner wisdom and autonomy.

For clients stuck in reliving their past traumas, The Work offers a lifeline—a way to process pain and begin releasing it finally. The simple act of questioning trauma's negative legacy can become the first courageous step toward reclaiming power and living more fully.

The Work's application extends beyond the individual to the collective realm. You can utilize its framework in individual or group therapy settings to help clients foster understanding across differences, facilitating true perspective-taking. Imagine clients stuck in prejudice gaining the skills to question their assumptions, cultivating openness and compassion.

One of the most compelling aspects of The Work is its versatility across diverse demographics, backgrounds, and mental health issues. Let it become your Swiss Army knife for change, customizing it to enhance your current approach. Even clients with severe pathology can experience breakthroughs through The Work when applied judiciously.

This journey also holds revolutionary potential for your development as a therapist. Make The Work part of your practice to reignite passion and purpose, promote self-awareness, and continually hone your clinical skills. You will soon discover that The Work offers a dual path of professional and personal growth.

While still in its early stages, empirical research reveals promising qualitative and quantitative evidence about The Work's benefits. Become part of the pioneering group of therapists who are rigorously studying its effects. With an open and curious mindset, imagine the frontiers we can cross together.

Finally, consider how The Work aligns with a paradigm focused not solely on thought content but on cultivating the aware space behind such thoughts. Here, it integrates seamlessly with mindfulness-based and Buddhist-inspired psychology. This integrative approach presents exciting possibilities for synthesis.

I hope this book has ignited your curiosity about the potential of The Work and how you might incorporate its transformative power into your clinical practice. With an open mind and heart, you now hold the tools to guide you and your clients into richer realms of healing, insight, and human connection. The journey ahead promises to be deeply meaningful when traveled together. I wish you courage, compassion, and discovery along the way. Together, we can plant seeds of peace in the world, one question at a time.

Are you ready to introduce The Work into your clinical practice and create positive change? If so, I'd love to hear from you as you make these powerful techniques a part of your therapeutic skillset.

# BIBLIOGRAPHY

APA, (2021, Oct 19). *American Psychological Association.* Retrieved from Demand for mental health treatment continues to increase, say psychologists: https://www.apa.org/news/press/releases/2021/10/mental-health-treatment-demand.

Association, A. C. (2018). *American College Health Association-National College Health Assessment II: Undergraduate Student Reference Group Data Report Fall 2018.* Silver Spring, MD: AMerican College Health Association.

Erlebacher, A. &. (1969). Explanation of the Müller-Lyer illusion: confusion theory examined. *Journal of experimental psychology*, 462-467.

Farber, K. (2007). *The Art of Being Human.* Retrieved from The Art of Being Human: https://www.theartofbeinghuman.com/tw-and-ct.html.

Feldman, O. G.-A. (2021). Inquiry Based Stress Reduction (IBSR) improves overall stuttering experience among adults who stutter: A randomized controlled trial. *Journal of Clinical Medicine*, 2187.

Ferris France N, M. S.-F. (2019, February 14). *PLoS ONE.* Retrieved from PLoS ONE 14(2): e0210152: https://doi.org/10.1371/journal.pone.0210152.

Ferris France, N. M. (2015). "An unspoken world of unspoken things": a study identifying and exploring core beliefs underlying self-stigma among people living with HIV and AIDS in Ireland. *Swiss Medical Weekly*, 14113.

Ganz, A. personal communication, May 11, 2024.

Guzmán, M. (2022). *I never thought of it that way: How to have fearlessly curious conversations in dangerously divided times.* BenBella Books.

Jones, L. (2023). Genome-wide association study meta-analysis of suicide attempt identifies twelve genome-wide significant loci and implicates genetic risks for specific health factors. *The American Journal of Psychiatry*, 180 (10) 723-738.

Kaiser Family Foundation. (2023, March 20). *KFF.* Retrieved from The Implications of COVID-19 for Mental Health and Substance Use: https://www.kff.org/mental-health/issue-brief/the-implications-of-covid-19-for-mental-health-and-substance-use/.

Katie, B., & Katz, M. (2005). *I need your love—is that true?: how to stop seeking love, approval, and appreciation and start finding them instead.* New York: Three Rivers Press.

Katie, B., & Mitchell, S. (2002). *Loving what is: four questions that can change your life.* New York: Harmony Books.

Katie, B., & Mitchell, S. (2007). *A thousand names for joy: living in harmony with the way things are.* Harmony Books.

Katie, B., & Mitchell, S. (2017). *A mind at home with itself: how asking four questions can free your mind, open your heart, and turn your world around.* New York: Harper One.

Landau, C. N.-A. (2021). Effect of inquiry-based stress reduction on well-being and views on risk-reducing surgery among women with BRCA variants in Israel: A randomized clinical trial. *JAMA Network*, 39670.

Le-Ari, S et al, (2013). A prospective pilot clinical trial of "The Work" meditation technique for survivors of breast cancer. *European Journal of Integrative Medicine. Vol. 5, No. 6, pp. 487-494.*

Luff, J. &. (2017). *Exploring Inquiry-Based Stress Reduction (IBSR) as a Counselling Intervention. International Conference on Education, Psychology, and Social Sciences.*

Michl, L. C., McLaughlin, K. A., Shepherd, K., & Nolen-Hoeksema, S. (2013). Rumination as a mechanism linking stressful life events to symptoms of depression and anxiety: Longitudinal evidence in early adolescents and adults. *Journal of Abnormal Psychology, 122(2), 339–352.*

National Institute of Mental Health. (2023, May 22). *NIMH.* Retrieved from Youth Suicide Rates Increased During the COVID-19 Pandemic: https://www.nimh.nih.gov/news/science-news/2023/youth-suicide-rates-increased-during-the-covid-19-pandemic.

Ramakonar, H. F. (2011). The rubber hand illusion and its application to clinical neuroscience. *Journal of Clinical Neuroscience*, 1596-1601.

Schnaider-Levi L, Ganz AB, Zafrani K, Goldman Z, Mitnik I, Rolnik B, Lev-Ari S. The Effect of Inquiry-Based Stress Reduction on Teacher Burnout: A Controlled Trial. *Brain Sci. 2020 Jul 21;10(7):468.*

Segal, Z. V. (2018). *Mindfulness-based cognitive therapy for depression (2nd ed.).* New York City: Guilford Press.

Smernoff, E. M.-A. (2015). The effects of "The Work" meditation (Byron Katie) on psychological symptoms and quality of life--a pilot clinical study. *Explore*, 24-31.

Tajnia, S. I. (2022). Investigating the effect of inquiry-based stress reduction on mortality awareness and interpersonal problems among intensive care unit nurses. *BMC Psychiatry*, 106.

US Surgeon General. (2021). *Protecting Youth Mental Health.* Retrieved from Health and Human Services: https://www.hhs.gov/sites/default/files/surgeon-general-youth-mental-health-advisory.pdf.

Zadok-Gurman, T. J.-A. (2021). Effect of Inquiry-Based Stress Reduction (IBSR) Intervention on Well-Being, Resilience and Burnout of Teachers during the COVID-19 Pandemic. *International Journal of Environmental Research and Public Health*, 3689.

www.ingramcontent.com/pod-product-compliance
Lightning Source LLC
LaVergne TN
LVHW052312200926
848481LV00002B/534